Praise for *The Cube and the Cathedral*

"An engagingly written book."—*Wall Street Journal*

"A finely honed reflection on post-Christian Europe."
—*Weekly Standard*

"A sumptuous banquet, stuffed with enough ideas for several
books. Even to summarize the argument is a formidable
task; Mr. Weigel's prose is so rich."—*New York Sun*

"Mr. Weigel is a past master at penning lively and lucid
studies of contemporary issues."—*National Catholic
Reporter*

"Readers given to pondering European affairs will find much
to pique thoughtful discussion."—*Publishers Weekly*

"Weigel's pithy polemic boldly assesses contemporary
Europe. . . Sure to be much discussed—and possibly to be
remarkably influential."—*Kirkus Reviews*

"Weigel has a nuanced and restrained vision for the role
religion should have in public life—for him, it should be a
strong and welcomed voice in democratic debates, but not a
voice that drowns out all others. . . thoroughly readable."
—*Tulsa World*

"A brisk look at the state of European culture and
politics."—*Washington Times*

"George Weigel's impassioned essay on the strange death of European Christianity is at once an elegy and a warning—an elegy for a venerable culture that is being effaced by a vacuous secularism, and a warning to Americans that their assumptions about a shared 'Western civilization' are fast becoming obsolete on the Eastern side of the Atlantic."
—**Niall Ferguson, author of *Empire* and *Collossus***

"In this elegant and highly readable book, George Weigel explains why Europe suddenly seems so distant from America, and why Americans have to be concerned with modern Europe's flight from politics, its demographic crisis, and its willful forgetfulness of its civilizational roots. One hopes that Weigel's book, like Tocqueville's reflections on America, will find a wide audience among those to whom he has held up a mirror. *The Cube and the Cathedral* is George Weigel at his best—learned yet sprightly, deeply serious yet buoyantly hopeful."—**Mary Ann Glendon, Learned Hand Professor of Law, Harvard University**

The Cube

and the

Cathedral

The Cube
and the
Cathedral

Europe, America, and
Politics Without God

GEORGE WEIGEL

BASIC
BOOKS

A MEMBER OF THE
PERSEUS BOOKS GROUP
NEW YORK

Hardcover edition first published in 2005 by Basic Books,
A Member of the Perseus Books Group

Paperback edition first published in 2006 by Basic Books.

Books published by Basic Books are available at special discounts for bulk
purchases in the United States by corporations, institutions, and other
organizations. For more information, please contact the Special Markets
Department at the Perseus Books Group, 11 Cambridge Center, Cambridge,
MA 02142, or call (617) 252-5298 or (800) 255-1514, or e-mail
special.markets@perseusbooks.com.

Cataloging-in-publication data for this book is available from the
Library of Congress.

Hardcover: ISBN-13: 978-0-465-09266-6; ISBN 10: 0-465-09266-7
Paperback: ISBN 13: 978-0-465-09268-0; ISBN 10: 0-465-09268-3

06 07 08 / 10 9 8 7 6 5 4 3 2 1

Amicis Cracoviensibus Meis In Corde Europae

Questions Atop the Cube

At the far western end of the axis that traverses Paris from the Louvre down the Champs Elysées and through the Arc de Triomphe, crossing the Seine at the Pont de Neuilly, is La Grande Arche de la Défense—like the more famous Pompidou Center, one of the *grands projets* of the late French president, François Mitterrand. Designed by Johann Otto von Spreckelsen, a Danish architect of sternly modernist sensibility, La Grande Arche is a colossal open cube: almost 40 stories tall, 348 feet wide, faced in glass and 2.47 acres of white Carrara marble. On a hot, sunny afternoon in August 1997, which is when I first saw it, La Grande Arche can be, quite literally, dazzling. A lift, definitely not for those inclined to vertigo, whisks the visitor up to a rooftop terrace, which offers an unparalleled view of the French capital, past the Tuilleries to the Louvre and on to the Île de la Cité, Sainte Chapelle, and Notre-Dame.

The arch's three-story-high roof also houses the International Foundation for Human Rights. For François Mitterrand intended La Grande Arche as a human rights monument, something suitably gigantic to mark the bicentenary of the French Revolution and the Declaration of the Rights of Man and Citizen. Thus, in one guidebook, La Grande Arche was dubbed "Fraternity Arch." That same guidebook, like every other one I consulted, emphasized that the entire Cathedral of Notre-Dame—towers and spire included—would fit comfortably inside the Great Arch.

All of which raised some questions in my mind, as I walked along the terrace admiring one of the world's great cityscapes. Which culture, I wondered, would better protect human rights? Which culture would more firmly secure the moral foundations of democracy? The culture that built this stunning, rational, angular, geometrically precise but essentially featureless cube? Or the culture that produced the vaulting and bosses, the gargoyles and flying buttresses, the nooks and crannies, the asymmetries and holy "unsameness" of Notre-Dame and the other great Gothic cathedrals of Europe?

More Questions

Those questions have come back to me, time and
again, as I've tried to understand what has happened in
Europe—and what has happened *to* western Europe in
particular—in recent decades: when I try to understand
why Europe's approach to democracy and to the responsibilities of the democracies in world politics seems
so different from many Americans' understanding of
these issues. In the first years of the twenty-first century, and at a moment in history when the democratic
ideal had energized much of the world, Americans suddenly seemed to be approaching a parting of the ways
with many of our European friends in understanding
the democratic project—its sources, its possibilities,

and the threats to it. As an American acutely aware of the debt of gratitude my country owes to Europe, a widening rift between the United States and the countries and cultures from which America was born did not strike me as a happy prospect.

And still the questions came. They were intensified in the wake of 9/11, when, after an initial period of European solidarity with the United States, fundamental differences arose between the United States and its oldest allies on the question of how best to respond to the threat posed by international terrorism, especially terrorism that claimed a religious sanction from Islam. Yet as I explored these problems with European friends from both the long-established democracies of western Europe and the new democracies of east central Europe, it struck me that the rift between the United States and Europe on, say, the best means to disarm the Saddam Hussein regime in Iraq touched only the surface of things.

How, for example, should one understand the fierce argument in Europe over whether a new constitutional treaty for the expanding European Union should include a reference to the Christian sources of European civilization? Why were so many European intellectuals and political leaders determined, or so it seemed, to airbrush fifteen hundred years of European history from their collective memory? Why did those same intellectuals and politicians deem any reference to the Christian sources of contemporary Europe's commitments to human rights and democracy a profound threat to human rights and democracy? Was there some connection between this internal European debate over Europe's constitution-making and the events that caught the attention of American headline writers and TV news anchormen—the harsh words between Europeans and Americans over Iraq; the portrait in the European press of Americans (and especially an American president) as religious fanatics intent on shooting up the world; the vastly different respect afforded the United Nations by Europeans and Americans?

These phenomena, I suggest, are related. Understanding them requires something more than a conventional political analysis. Political answers alone cannot account for what seems, from the western side of the Atlantic, Europe's crankiness—whether that crankiness be about the democracies' struggle against terrorism or the structures and processes of European integration. Nor can political answers alone explain the reasons behind perhaps the most urgent issue confronting Europe today—the fact that western Europe is committing a form of demographic suicide, its far below replacement-level birthrates creating enormous pressures on the European welfare state and a demographic vacuum into which Islamic immigrants are flowing in increasing numbers, often becoming radicalized in the process.

In the aftermath of 9/11, and especially during the debate that preceded and followed the Iraq War of 2003–2004, Americans became acutely aware that they have a "Europe problem." So, I have discovered, do some Europeans, including European intellectuals. My proposal—which in retrospect had its origins in my meditations atop the Grande Arche de la Défense—is that the "Europe problem" is best understood in moral and cultural terms. My further proposal is that this "problem," while it presents itself most acutely in western Europe, is not just one besetting America's European friends and allies. Their "Europe problem" is—or could be—America's problem too.

The "Europe problem," as I have come to think of it, is fundamentally a problem of cultural and civilizational morale. Over it hovers the question posed sharply, if unintentionally, by guidebooks that boast about the alleged superiority of La Grande Arche to Notre-Dame: the question of the cube and the cathedral, and their relationship to both the meaning of freedom and the future of democracy.

Martians and Venusians?

A widely discussed American analysis of America's Europe problem and Europe's America problem was advanced by Robert Kagan in *Of Paradise and Power: America and Europe in the New World Order* (2003).[1] Using a popular trope that he may have subsequently come to view with a bit of chagrin, Kagan argues that "on major strategic and international questions today, Americans are from Mars and Europeans are from Venus."[2] However fetching such a characterization may be in a sound bite world, it does scant justice to the seriousness of Kagan's argument.

To begin with, Kagan understands that not all Europeans are "from Venus"—Tony Blair comes to mind—

nor are all Americans "from Mars." Yet Kagan insists that these stereotypes—Americans are from Mars, Europeans from Venus—disclose important truths. The United States and western Europe have different strategic visions: different understandings of how the world works, different understandings of the nature of power, different understandings of the causes of conflict in the world, different views of the role of international legal and political organizations in managing conflict, and different perceptions of the utility of military power in securing peace, freedom, and order in world affairs— and that's *before* we get to the policy differences that separate the United States and Europe on issues such as the path to peace in the Middle East, the International Criminal Court, the rebuilding of Iraq, and so forth.

Kagan suggests that these dramatically different strategic visions are not the by-products of national character, reminding us of Europe's bellicose past and America's traditional nervousness about international power politics and entangling alliances. Rather, on Kagan's view, these different strategic visions are the product of a great disparity of military power between the United States and Europe. That power gap did not just happen, though; the disparity in military power between the U.S. and Europe is itself the product of an ideological gap between the older, established democracies of western Europe and the United States—what Kagan terms "a different set of ideals and principles regarding the utility and morality of power."[3] The ideological gap in turn is based on a different set of experiences in the twentieth century.

The European Continent's devastation by two world wars; its division during a Cold War that, had it broken out into hot war, would likely have destroyed Europe; the longer European experience of vulnerability to terrorism—all of this, Kagan suggests, led Europeans to a different set of perceptions about the threats to peace and freedom at work in the twenty-first-century world. Moreover, these experiences led many prominent Europeans to the conviction that security threats can and should be met, in the main, not by traditional applications of military "hard power," but by the further refinement of international legal and political instruments of conflict resolution. The most enthusiastic European "Venusians," like European Commission president and former Italian prime minister Romano Prodi, see the present European Union as the model, indeed the prefiguration, of a world run by "soft power." As Prodi put it in a May 2001 speech in Paris, in Europe, "the rule of law has replaced the crude interplay of power . . . power politics have lost their influence; [therefore, by] making a success of [European] integration we are demonstrating to the world that it is possible to create a method for peace."[4] This, Kagan suggests, has become Europe's new *mission civilisatrice*, its civilizing mission: Europe is to bring to the world the fulfillment of Immanuel Kant's vision of perpetual peace.[5]

Kagan understands that Europe's passion for this new mission is in part a function of the fear that dare not speak its name—that if the experience of an integrated, peaceful, post–Cold War Europe *isn't* universalizable, then it might not be a settled accomplishment for Europe, either. And that is to think the unthinkable in circumstances in which, as Kagan puts it, "the French are still not confident they can trust the Germans, and the Germans are still not sure they can trust themselves."[6] That, in turn, helps explain why Europe's integration—intended by some to create a European superpower and an independent European foreign and defense policy—has gone hand in hand with a drastic decline, absolutely and relatively, in Europe's "hard power" capabilities.

There are many ironies in the fire here, and Kagan neatly sums them up:

Europe's rejection of power politics, its devaluing of military force as a tool of international relations, have depended on the presence of American military forces on European soil. Europe's new Kantian order could flourish only under the umbrella of American power exercised according to the rules of the old Hobbesian order. American power made it possible for Europeans to believe that power was no longer important. And now, in the final irony, the fact that United States military power has solved the European problem, especially the "German question," allows Europeans today to believe that American military power, and the "strategic culture" that has created and sustained it, are outmoded and dangerous.[7]

And that, in Kagan's view, leads to the "great paradox," namely, that Europe's emergence into posthistory has been made possible by the fact that the United States still lives *in* history: "Because Europe has neither the will nor the ability to guard its own paradise and keep it from being overrun, spiritually as well as physically, by a world that has yet to accept the rule of 'moral consciousness,' it has become dependent on America's willingness to use its military might to deter or defeat those around the world who still believe in power politics."[8]

Which brief summary of his position will, I hope, drive home the point that Dr. Kagan does his argument insufficient justice when he reduces it to a matter of Martians versus Venusians.

True, but Insufficient

Yet for all its insight into why Europeans and Americans see the world and world politics so differently, Robert Kagan's analysis does not get us to the roots of the matter. Yes, western Europeans have ordered their institutions, their politics, and their national budgets according to a distinctive understanding of how the twenty-first century works—or should work. Yes, that different vision of the world and its possibilities is the product of experiences unlike those Americans underwent in the twentieth century. Yes, Europeans can find some historical warrant for believing that a world of perpetual peace is possible in Kant's idealism (and I mean "idealism" in both its philosophical and psychological senses).

But why did Europe turn out this way? Why did Europeans learn these things from their experience? And why have these lessons taken the political and ideological forms they have?

German commentator Josef Joffe and French political theorist Alain Finkielkraut get us a bit closer to an answer by focusing on the trauma of Europe's mid–twentieth century, the years when Europe seemed to lose its mind and its way. As Joffe wrote in late 2003, in an essay attempting to parse the antipathy many European intellectuals and activists feel toward both the United States and Israel, "Much of Western Europe has drawn its post-Holocaust identity from the rejection of the darkest part of the Continent's proud history. The battle cry of postwar Europe is 'Never Again!,' as Alain Finkielkraut has put it: a 'no' to fuehrers, duces, and caudillos, to colonialism, conquest, and discrimination against the 'Other.' To regain moral stature, Europeans have turned antifascism into a doctrine of worldly transcendence, with a secular decalogue that reads, in part: thou shalt not pray to the discredited gods of nationalism; thou shalt not practice power politics; thou shalt relinquish sovereignty and rejoice in cooperation."[9]

This is, as I say, closer to the heart of the matter: the embrace of the "end of politics" trumpeted by Romano Prodi and others is, in some part, a mundane quest for absolution from Europe's guilt at having produced the Holocaust (not to mention the Gulag, the Ukrainian terror famine, the Spanish Civil War, and World War I, which set the whole bloody business in motion). But why is this search for historical absolution ultramundane, so to speak? Moreover, does a political–psychological analysis about projected guilt over the Holocaust (and the rest of the parade of horribles) get us to the roots of what thoughtful Europeans and concerned Americans alike perceive as Europe's present malaise? I don't find that answer satisfactory in trying to understand certain other prominent, and disturbing, features of recent European life. Neither do some of my European friends.

Puzzles

❖ Why, in the aftermath of 1989, did Europeans fail to condemn communism as a moral and political monstrosity? Why was the only politically acceptable judgment on communism the anodyne observation that it "didn't work"?

❖ Why, to come to the present, do European statesmen insist on defending certain fictions in world politics: like the fiction that Yasser Arafat was interested in peace with Israel; or the fiction that the Kyoto protocol on climate change would be rigorously observed by the nations that signed the Kyoto agreement; or the fiction that the leaders of Iran are to be taken at their word when they pledge not to develop nuclear weapons; or the fiction that there is something meaningfully describable in *political* terms as an "international community," the highest expression of which is the U.N. Security Council as presently configured?

❖ What accounts for Europe's fideism, its will to believe, about international organizations? Why, as historian John Keegan put it, did Europeans in the early twenty-first century often espouse "a philosophy of international action that actually rejected action and took refuge in the belief that all conflicts of interest were to be settled by consultation, conciliation, and the intervention of international agencies"?[10]

❖ What accounts for disturbing currents of irrationality in contemporary European politics? Why did one of every five Germans (and one-third of those under 30) believe that the United States was responsible for 9/11, while some 300,000 French men and women made a best-seller out of *L'Effroyable imposture* (The Appalling Fraud), in which the author, Thierry Meyssan, argued that the Twin Towers of the World Trade Center were destroyed by the U.S. military, using remote-controlled airliners?[11] Why did a rock concert crowd in Dublin in June 2004 applaud when Morrissey, an aging pop singer, announced the death of Ronald Reagan? Why did he receive an even larger ovation when he said that he only wished it had been George W. Bush who had died?[12] Why did 25 percent of the French (and 30 percent of those under 35) tell pollsters that they wanted Saddam Hussein, an acknowledged mass murderer, to win the Iraq War?[13]

❖ Why did voters in Spain give a de facto victory to appeasement in their March 2004 elections, days after al Qaeda operatives killed hundreds and wounded thousands by bombing a Madrid train station?

❖ Why is European productivity dwindling? Why does Germany, rightly renowned as the economic engine of the European Union, have a per capita gross domestic product equivalent to Arkansas and only slightly higher than West Virginia and Mississippi? Why does Sweden have a considerably higher level of its population living below the poverty line (calculated at an annual household income of $25,000) than the United States?[14]

❖ Why, in the process of enlarging the European Union, is Europe retreating from democracy and binding itself ever more tightly in the cords of bureaucracy, with Brussels bureaucrats calculating the appropriate circumference of tomatoes and prescribing the proper feeding procedures for Sardinian hogs?

❖ Why do European states find it virtually impossible to make hard domestic political decisions—as on the length of the work week or the funding of pensions?

❖ Why do European courts seek an expanded international jurisdiction that defies the democratically agreed-to arrangements made by free people in other countries (as in the Pinochet case, when a Spanish judge sought to overturn the democratic decision of the people of Chile about the fate of the former dictator)?

❖ Why is Europe on the way to what French political philosopher Pierre Manent calls "depoliticization?" Why, as Manent puts it, does Europe "[drug] itself with humanitarianism in order to forget that it exists less and less politically"? Why does Manent have "the impression today that the greatest ambition of Europeans is to become the inspectors of American prisons"?[15]

❖ Why are so many European public intellectuals "Christophobic," as international legal scholar J. H. H. Weiler (himself an observant Jew) puts it? Why are crude caricatures of Christianity (the Eucharist mocked on television as a "religious snack," Christ on the cross depicted as a dispenser of toilet paper) tolerated in European popular culture in a way that similar defamations of Judaism and Islam would never be?[16] Why did so many of Europe's political leaders insist that the new constitution for Europe include a deliberate act of historical amnesia, in which a millennium and a half of Christianity's contributions to European understandings of human rights and democracy were deliberately ignored—indeed, denied?

❖ Why, in addition to its "Christophobia," is European high culture so enamored of the present and so contemptuous of both religious and secular tradition, as French philosopher Rémi Brague has pointed out? What accounts for this cult of the contemporary?[17]

❖ Why do certain parts of Europe exhibit a curious, even bizarre, approach to death? Why did so many of the French prefer to continue their summer vacations during the European heat wave of 2003, leaving their parents unburied and warehoused in refrigerated lockers (which were soon overflowing)? Why is death increasingly anonymous in Germany, with no death notice in the newspapers, no church funeral ceremony, no secular memorial service—"as though," Richard John Neuhaus observed, "the deceased did not exist"? What are we to make of the Swedish company Promessa, which advertises a service in which cremation is replaced with human composting, the dead being immersed and frozen in liquid nitrogen before being smashed to smithereens by ultrasound waves and then freeze-dried and used for fertilizer?[18]

❖ Above all, and most urgently of all, why is Europe committing demographic suicide, systematically depopulating itself in what British historian Niall Ferguson calls the greatest "sustained reduction in European population since the Black Death of the 14th century"?[19]

- Why do eighteen European countries report "negative natural increase" (i.e., more deaths than births)?[20]
- Why does no western European country have a replacement-level birthrate? (The replacement level, according to demographers, is 2.1 children per woman; as of 2004, Germany's birthrate was 1.3, Italy's 1.2, Spain's 1.1, and

France's 1.7; the higher French rate is due to Muslim immigration).[21]*

- Why is Germany likely to lose the equivalent of the population of the former East Germany in the first half of the 21st century?[22]
- Why will Spain's population decline from 40 million to 31.3 million by the middle of the century?
- Why will 42 percent of Italians be over sixty by 2050—at which point, on present trends, almost 60 percent of the Italian people will have no brothers, sisters, cousins, aunts, or uncles?[23]
- Why will Europe's retired population increase by 55 percent in the next twenty-five years, while its working population will shrink by 8 percent—and, to repeat, why can't Europeans, either politicians or the public, draw the obvious conclusions from these figures about the impending bankruptcy of their social welfare, health care, and pension systems? Why, to cite Niall Ferguson again, is Europe's "fundamental problem . . . senescence"?[24]

---

*As demographer Nicholas Eberstadt has noted, the difference between a replacement-level birthrate and a birthrate of 1.5 or 1.4, other things being equal, is the difference between a stable population over time and a population that decreases by one-third as each generation passes.

- What is happening when an entire continent, wealthier and healthier than ever before, declines to create the human future in the most elemental sense, by creating a next generation?
- Why do many Europeans deny that these demographics—which are without parallel in human history, absent wars, plagues, or natural catastrophes—are the defining reality of their twenty-first century?[25]

These questions cannot be answered satisfactorily by reference only to Europe's distinct experience of the twentieth century and what Europe learned from it. Nor can they be answered by appeals to European shame. A deeper question has to be raised: *Why did Europe have the twentieth century it did?* Why did a century that began with confident predictions about a maturing humanity reaching new heights of civilizational accomplishment produce in Europe, within four decades, two world wars, three totalitarian systems, a Cold War threatening global catastrophe, oceans of blood, mountains of corpses, Auschwitz and the Gulag? What happened? Why?

A Disclaimer

Writing about the dramatic change in relations between the United States and Europe, John Keegan observes that "America was able to count on many allies in the Western world" during the Cold War. But most of those allies "proved fair-weather friends" after the collapse of European communism and the Soviet crack-up.[26] However true that may or may not be—and I'm inclined to think that Keegan is being a little harsh—I want to emphasize that my questions about Europe and my concerns for its crisis of civilizational morale are not the questions and concerns of a betrayed friend, embittered by a lack of gratitude on the part of former allies. Nor am I primarily concerned by the adjustment of interests and alliances that usually follows epochal historical change, such as the Revolution of 1989 and the Soviet collapse of 1991. Other American observers of Europe may be motivated primarily by feelings of unrequited brotherhood. Still others may have been jarred by recent reminders that states have no permanent alliances, only permanent interests. I am neither.

Moreover, no American aware of the defects of his own country would suggest—and I am emphatically *not* suggesting—that the United States has achieved a state of social, economic, cultural, and political perfection that can only lead Americans to look with dismay at Europe's decline and decay. There is plenty to be worried about in the United States: a regime of legalized abortion in which an endangered species of bird in a national forest enjoys more legal protection in America than a six-month-old unborn child; too widespread and ready a resort to capital punishment; cultural vulgarities of various sorts (including the global export of pornography via the Internet); legislative logjams on crucial issues like the fiscal rescue of Social Security or the regulation of the new biotechnologies; high rates of divorce and out-of-wedlock births; an inability to debate issues like the meaning of marriage or the ethics of embryo research in terms other than the sentimental or the utilitarian; the continued sway of political correctness (and the consequent stifling of free speech and serious argument) in too many institutions of higher education; courts usurping the prerogatives of legislatures; the enforcement of a soft secularism in public life; and so forth and so on. The list could obviously be expanded.

And while some things in the United States are in fact getting better—welfare reform seems to have worked; the adjustment from an industrial to a postindustrial economy has gone relatively smoothly, indeed far more smoothly than the transition from the preindustrial to the industrial world; racial attitudes in America are more egalitarian than in any other developed society, as a result of a striking moral and cultural revolution begun in the mid-1950s; charitable giving continues to climb and voluntarism is robust; opportunity remains open to virtually anyone willing to study, work, and save, as the country's continuing absorption and mainstreaming of immigrants attests—there is probably no example of a European problem cited above for which one couldn't find a parallel example in the United States. "They" have Thierry Meyssan; "we" have Michael Moore. And so on.

The difference, I suggest, is that Pierre Manent's depoliticization is far more advanced in Europe than in the United States. And that has happened for a reason: a reason having to do with European secularism, a phenomenon that may also shed light on Europe's impending demographic catastrophe. In brief, while the United States may eventually be headed for a crisis of civilizational morale, Europe is *in* such a crisis today. And that crisis may have something to do with the further great difference between the United States and Europe, which touches the problem Joseph Weiler calls "Christophobia."

Whatever else you can say about the United States, it is most certainly not a Christophobic or post-Christian society. European high culture is largely Christophobic, and Europeans themselves describe their cultures and societies as post-Christian. It would be too simple to say that the reason Americans and Europeans see the world so differently is that the former go to church on Sundays and the latter don't. But it would also be a grave mistake to think that the dramatic differences in religious belief and practice in the United States and Europe don't have something important to do with those different perceptions of the world—and the different policies to which those perceptions eventually lead.

Probing to the deeper, subsurface roots of Europe's crisis of civilizational morale is not only important for understanding Europe today and for discerning what-ever promising paths of European renewal there may be aborning—although those are important things. Getting at the roots of "Europe's problem" is also im-portant for understanding a set of problems Americans may face in the not-too-distant future. Their "Europe problem" could be ours, someday. If we wish to avoid that fate, we would do well to learn from the experience of those who were, throughout the twentieth century, our closest allies in the cause of freedom.

That learning might begin in the new democracies of central and eastern Europe, where history and its dynamics look different—at least as compared to the view from Berlin, Brussels, London, Paris, or Vienna.

What Makes History Go?

Over the course of thirteen years of research and teaching in east central Europe, I've been impressed by what might be called the Slavic view of history. You can find it in a great thinker who lived in the borderland between Orthodoxy and Catholicism, Vladimir Soloviev, with his religious and moral challenge to the fashionable nihilism and materialism of the late nineteenth century. You can find it in the Polish novelist Henryk Sienkiewicz, and in the poets and playwrights of Polish Romanticism—Adam Mickiewicz, Juliusz Słowacki, Cyprian Kamil Norwid—who broke decisively with the Jacobin conviction, born in France in 1789, that revolution meant a complete rupture with the past; by contrast, the Poles insisted that genuine revolution meant the recovery of lost spiritual and moral values. You can find it in Karol Wojtyła, the late Pope John Paul II, and in such intellectual leaders of the anticommunist resistance in east central Europe as Václav Havel and Václav Benda, who all believed that "living in the truth" could change what seemed un-changeable in history.[27]

The common thread running through these dis-parate thinkers is the conviction that the deepest cur-rents of history are spiritual and cultural, rather than political and economic. In this way of thinking, history is not simply the by-product of the contest for power in the world—although power plays an important role in history. And history is certainly not the exhaust fumes produced by the means of production, as the Marxists taught. Rather, history is driven, over the long haul, by culture—by what men and women honor, cherish, and worship; by what societies deem to be true and good and noble; by the expressions they give to those convictions in language, literature, and the arts; by what individuals and societies are willing to stake their lives on.

Poland is one embodiment of this way of thinking, which Poles believe has been vindicated empirically by

their own modern history. In 1795, with the Third Polish Partition, the great powers of the region—Russia,
Prussia, Austria—completed the vivisection of a political community whose origins went back to the last
years of the first millennium of Christian history; thus
for 123 years, from 1795 to 1918, the Polish state was
erased from Europe. Yet during that century and a
quarter in which you could not find "Poland" on any
map of Europe—a time in which the Russians and
Prussians, in particular, made strenuous efforts to erad-
icate the idea of "Poland"—the Polish nation survived.
Indeed, the Polish nation survived with such vigor that
it could give birth to a new Polish state in 1918. And
despite the fact that the revived Polish state was then
beset for fifty years by the plagues of Nazism and communism, the Polish nation proved strong enough to
give a new birth to freedom in east central Europe in
the Revolution of 1989.

How did this happen? Poland survived—better,
Poland prevailed—because of culture: a culture formed
by a distinctive language (Slavic, yet written in a Lati-
nate alphabet and thus oriented to the West as well as
the East); by a unique literature, which helped keep
alive the memory and idea of "Poland"; and by the in-
tensity of its Catholic faith (which, in its noblest and

deepest expressions, was ecumenical and tolerant, not xenophobic, as so many stereotypes have it). Poles know in their bones that culture is what drives history over the long haul.

To call this a "Slavic view of history" reflects the principal location of this body of thought over the past two hundred years or so. In fact, though, it is really a classically Christian way of thinking about history, whose roots can be traced back at least as far as St. Augustine and *The City of God*. In the English-speaking world of the twentieth century, the most distinguished exponent of this culture-driven view of history was Christopher Dawson. As Dawson once put it in one of the most cited passages from his voluminous body of work, St. Paul's passage from Troy in Asia Minor to Philippi on the European mainland did more to shape the future of European culture and European history than anything recorded about that place and time by Livy and the other great historians of his day. Granted, Paul's crossing over to Philippi took place "underneath the surface" of history, such that those who even noticed that an itinerant rabbi from Tarsus had come to Europe and was preaching another king than Caesar couldn't grasp the significance of what was being said. But its invisibility to those writing history in the first century A.D. was, it turned out, no true measure of what was really important for the human future in the affairs of first century Asia Minor.[28]

In any case, it is the Slavs who have been, in our time, the most powerful exponents of this culture-first understanding of the dynamics of the world's story. One such Slavic reader of the signs of the times, Aleksandr Solzhenitsyn, brought this optic on history to bear on the "Europe problem" in his 1983 Templeton Prize Lecture. Parsing the horrors of the twentieth century, Solzhenitsyn found a historical trapgate in World War I:

> The failings of human consciousness, deprived of its divine dimension, have been a determining factor in all the major crimes of this century. The first of these was World War I, and much of our present predicament can be traced back to it. That war . . . took place when Europe, bursting with health and abundance, fell into a rage of self-mutilation that could not but sap its strength for a century or more, and perhaps forever. The only possible explanation for this is a mental eclipse among the leaders of Europe due to their lost awareness of a Supreme Power above them. . . . Only the loss of that higher intuition which comes from God could have allowed the West to accept calmly, after World War I, the protracted agony of Russia as she was being torn apart by a band of cannibals. . . . The West did not

perceive that this was in fact the beginning of a lengthy process that spells disaster for the whole world.[29]

As the twentieth century gave way to the twenty-first, the disaster Solzhenitsyn foresaw had been avoided, at least in the form of nuclear holocaust. But that does not diminish the salience of Solzhenitsyn's chief point—that 1914–1918 marked the beginning of a civilizational crisis in Europe, and perhaps especially in western Europe, whose effects are much with us today. Indeed, in trying to get a satisfactory answer to several of the questions I raised above, including the critical question of Europe's demographic self-immolation, I can think of no better answer than the one suggested by Solzhenitsyn's analysis: these phenomena are the expression of a profound, long-standing crisis of civilizational morale.

The Trapgate of 1914

The new World War II Memorial on the Mall in Washington, D.C., bears witness to the fact that most Americans—like, I expect, most Europeans—think of the Second World War as the pivot on which the twentieth century turned. Yet the more one thinks about that bloodiest of centuries, which combined remarkable advances in human achievement with unprecedented eruptions of human wickedness, World War II comes into clearer focus as the midway point in a civilizational emergency that lasted more than three-quarters of a century: a crisis that began in August 1914, when the German army crashed through neutral Belgium en route to France, and was only concluded in August

1991, when the Soviet Union collapsed under western pressure, the weight of its own implausibility, and the demands of the peoples of the Soviet empire for national freedom. World War I, which was once known as the Great War, was precisely that: the great event that set the twentieth century on its distinctive course.

Some have accused Aleksandr Solzhenitsyn of succumbing to a bad habit occasionally found in other Russian thinkers—the tendency to blame all Russia's problems on others, rather than on Russia's own flaws and incapacities. Perhaps he has done that on occasion. But it seems to me that the great Russian witness to the horrors of the Gulag Archipelago is on to something important in his analysis of the Great War's impact on European culture and politics. Moreover, Solzhenitsyn is not alone in seeing August 1914 as the breakpoint, the moment when European civilization began to destroy itself.

Sir Edward Grey, Great Britain's foreign secretary at the time, was a Liberal who believed in progress; yet it was Grey who is famously said to have remarked, on the night of August 3, 1914, "The lamps are going out all over Europe; we shall not see them lit again in our lifetime."[30] Winston Churchill, a former soldier who thoroughly enjoyed his position as civilian chief of the British navy, had an intuition similar to the more pacific Grey's; writing his wife, Clementine, on July 29, 1914, Churchill warned that "everything tends toward catastrophe and collapse" as a "wave of madness has swept the mind of Christendom."[31]

If there is a flaw in Solzhenitsyn's reading of the historic trapgate that was August 1914, it may be in his too anodyne reading of Europe's prewar state of mind and soul. In a fresh analysis of the origins of the Great War, historian David Fromkin stresses that the arms race that preceded the Great War "took place in a civilization in which it was widely believed that only destruction could bring regeneration." The nihilist philosopher Friedrich Nietzsche, in other words, was the true prophet of the age aborning in the early years of the twentieth century; and Nietzsche was, Fromkin insists, a "European figure, not a parochial German one"—a man whose influence extended throughout the Continent, and who lived in Italy and Switzerland as well as Germany. Fromkin sums up the prewar cultural situation in a way that corrects aspects of Solzhenitsyn's historical portrait of pre–1914 Europe without contradicting Solzhenitsyn's basic point:

> In the opening years of the 20th century, Europeans glorified violence, and certain groups among them, at least, felt a need for radical change. Across the whole

spectrum of existence, change was overcoming Europe at a pace faster than ever before—and far faster than Europe knew how to cope with. A panoramic view of Europe in the years 1900 to 1914 would show prominently that the Continent was racing ahead in a scientific, technological, and industrial revolution, powered by almost limitless energy that was transforming almost everything; that violence was endemic in the service of social, economic, political, class, ethnic, and national strife; that Europe focused its energies on an escalating, dizzying arms race on a scale that the world had never seen before; and that, in the center of the Continent's affairs, powerful, dynamic Germany had made strategic arrangements such that, if it went to war, it would bring almost all Europe and much of the rest of the planet into the war for or against it.

Given these conditions, does not the question, "How could war have broken out in such a peaceful world?" rather answer itself? Would it not have been more to the point to ask how statesmen could have continued to avoid war much longer? How had they managed to keep the peace for so long? Which is not to say that war could *not* have been averted, but merely that, by 1914, it might have taken extraordinary skill to keep on averting it . . . in a world in which war was considered desirable—even necessary.[32]

Europe's passions brought the Continent to war in August 1914—the Nietzschean will to power; a distorted sense of honor; intense nationalism compounded by imperialism; the breakdown of the system of trust (and the erosion of the true meaning of honor) that had been the human and moral glue of European diplomacy in the preceding century; ethnic and racial stereotypes turned into the basis of Great Power policy. These passions also explain what seems even more incomprehensible: the continuation of the war, which quickly decayed into a meat grinder of endless slaughter in which generals sent soldiers to stop machine-gun bullets with their chests, after gridlock was reached in France in mid-September 1914, in the aftermath of the First Battle of the Marne. Reading John Keegan's *History of the First World War* some years ago while on a train trip through parts of the old German and Austro-Hungarian empires, I came to the point where the trench lines had been defined, mere weeks after the war's inception. Knowing what was coming, I could only ask myself, "Why didn't anyone say *Stop!?*" Why was there no one with the will, the authority, or the moral imagination and courage to pull the emergency brake as the train of European civilization headed for a catastrophic crash?

David Fromkin's description of the cast of mind in European high culture and among European political leaders in the first decades of the twentieth century not only suggests an answer to the question, Why did it happen? Fromkin's portrait of a civilization beset by destructive passions also helps answer the even more disturbing question, Why did it *continue?* Those of a secular cast of mind may object, in principle, to Aleksandr Solzhenitsyn's claim that it happened, and that it continued, because men had forgotten God. But they cannot object to the suggestion that men had forgotten something essential about their humanity—which may, as I hope to show later, have had more than a little to do with forgetting God.

World War I, the Great War, was the product of a crisis of civilizational morality, a failure of moral reason in a culture that had given the world the very concept of moral reason. That crisis of moral reason led to a crisis of civilizational morale that is much with us today.

It should not be surprising that this latter crisis has only become visible since the end of the Cold War. Its effects were first masked by the illusory peace that marked the period between World War I and World War II, then by the rise of totalitarianism and the Great Depression, then by the Second World War itself; and then by the Cold War. It was only after 1991, when the seventy-seven-year political–military crisis that began in 1914 had ended, that the long-term effects of Europe's "rage of self-mutilation" could come to the surface of history and be seen for what they were—and for what they are. Europe is experiencing a crisis of civilizational morale today because of what happened in Europe ninety years ago. That crisis couldn't be seen in its full and grave dimensions then, although figures ranging from Edward Grey and Winston Churchill to the German General Helmuth von Moltke, one of the chief instigators of the slaughter, knew that what was about to happen was desperately bad—a war, as Moltke put it on July 29, 1914, that would "annihilate the civilization of almost the whole of Europe for decades to come."[33] The damage done to the fabric of European culture and civilization in the Great War could only be seen clearly when the Great War's political effects had been cleared from the board in 1991. Recognizing that damage for what it was, and is, brings into sharper focus the "Europe problem" today.

Aleksandr Solzhenitsyn's insight into the meaning of the Great War reinforces the intuition that we should look to the realm of culture for a deeper explanation of the currents of history. And because the heart of culture is cult—what men and women cherish, honor, and worship—a theologically informed analysis of history may shed more light on what imagines itself to be the "real world" than other forms of analysis that imagine themselves more "realistic." Conventional political, economic, and historical analyses are unavailing, or at the very least unsatisfactory, in trying to understand the origins and nature of Europe's current situation—and why that crisis of civilizational morale may have important lessons in it for America, and indeed for the democratic project throughout the world.

So let's consider at least the possibility of reading history a very old-fashioned way—St. Augustine's way—through lenses ground by the tools of theology. That brings us to another Christian analyst of the dynamics of modern European history, who can help fill out Solzhenitsyn's indictment and help us imagine explanations of, and answers to, the "Europe problem" that cut more deeply than the political or psychological.

Something New: The Drama of Atheistic Humanism

Henri de Lubac, who died in 1991 at the ripe old age of ninety-five, was one of twentieth-century Catholicism's most distinguished and influential theologians. His voluminous writings touch topics ranging from the nature of divine revelation to the history of medieval biblical interpretation. During World War II, de Lubac was one of the principal contributors to *Cahiers du Témoignage chrétien* (Notebooks of Christian Witness). A crucial literary component of the French spiritual resistance to the Nazi occupation, *Témoignage chrétien* gave an underground voice to the persecuted Church and chronicled Catholic efforts to combat Nazi anti-Semitism. In the late 1940s and early 1950s, de Lubac came under the suspicion of some of the Church's Roman doctrinal watchdogs, nervous about his reinterpretation of medieval thinkers and his attempts to explain the supernatural to modern readers. But by the time of the Second Vatican Council (1962–1965), Father de Lubac had been "rehabilitated," and during the Council he played an important role in shaping one of Vatican II's most important documents, the *Pastoral Constitution on the Church and the Modern World*, often known by its Latin title, *Gaudium et Spes* (Joy and Hope). During the drafting of *Gaudium et Spes*, the French theologian worked closely with a young Polish archbishop, who became both a friend and an intellectual interlocutor; the Pole, Karol Wojtyła, would be elected pope in 1978. Five years later, Pope John Paul II broke centuries of precedent by making the now-retired Father Henri de Lubac a cardinal. (In a nice touch of papal whimsy, John Paul gave Cardinal de Lubac, as his Roman "parish," the church that had once been the "parish" of Cardinal Alfredo Ottaviani, de Lubac's Roman nemesis in the early 1950s.)[34]

Because of his penetrating insight into the Christian understanding of the world's possibilities and the world's demons, and because of the turbulence of the times in which he lived, Henri de Lubac's theology ventured far beyond the seminary lecture hall and the university seminar room to engage some of the most important moral and intellectual issues of the twentieth century. Like many other Europeans who had witnessed the Continent's travail during the first four and a half decades of a century that was supposed to produce a new flourishing of civilization, de Lubac was haunted by the question, *What happened?* Or, perhaps more to the point, *Why* had what happened, happened? His answer remains suggestive today—and sheds light, I think, on the "Europe problem" and its analogues in other parts of the western world, including the United States.

Throughout his long career, Father de Lubac was fascinated by the history of ideas, which he knew to be fraught with real-world repercussions. Thus, while France was occupied and de Lubac engaged in his resistance activities, he turned his attention to some of the most influential intellectual figures in pre–twentieth century European culture. The result was a book, *Le drame de l'humanisme athée* (1944), which argued that the civilizational crisis in which Europe found itself during World War II was the product of what he called atheistic humanism—the deliberate rejection of the God of the Bible, the God of Abraham, Isaac, Jacob, and Jesus, in the name of authentic human liberation.[35]

Here, de Lubac suggested, was a great reversal. In the classical world, and in the world of eastern Mediterranean paganism inhabited by the Jewish people as recorded in the Hebrew Bible, the gods, or Fate, played games with men and women, often with lethal consequences; remember the interference of the gods in human affairs in the *Iliad* and the *Odyssey*; or Israel's constant struggle against the practice of child sacrifice demanded by the gods of the Philistines and other neighboring nations. In the face of these experiences, the revelation of the God of the Bible—the self-disclosure in history of the one God who was neither a willful tyrant (to be avoided) nor a carnivorous predator (to be appeased) nor a remote abstraction (to be safely ignored)—was perceived as a great liberation. Human beings were not the playthings of the gods or the passive victims of Fate. And because they could have access to the one true God through prayer and worship, those who believed in the God of Abraham, Isaac, Jacob, and Jesus could bend history in a humane direction. History was not a stage on which human puppets were manipulated by gods and goddesses pulling the strings, so to speak. History was an arena of responsibility and purpose because history was the medium through which the one true God made himself known to his people and empowered them to lead lives of dignity, through the intelligence and free will with which he had endowed them in creation.

Yet what biblical man once perceived as liberation, the proponents of atheistic humanism perceived as bondage. Human freedom could not coexist with the God of Jews and Christians. Human greatness required rejecting the biblical God, according to atheistic humanism.

This, Father de Lubac argued, was something quite dramatically new. This was not the atheism of skeptical individuals looking to discomfort the neighbors or impress the faculty tenure committee. This was atheistic *humanism*—atheism with a developed ideology and a program for remaking the world. As a historian of ideas, de Lubac knew that ideas have consequences and that bad ideas can have lethal consequences. At the heart of the darkness inside the great mid–twentieth century tyrannies—communism, fascism, Nazism—Father de Lubac discerned the lethal effects of the marriage between modern technology and the culture-shaping ideas borne by atheistic humanism.

He summed up the results of this misbegotten union in the following terms: "It is not true, as is sometimes said, that man cannot organize the world without

God. What is true is that, without God, he can only organize it against man."[36] That is what the tyrannies of the mid–twentieth century had proven—ultramundane humanism is inevitably inhuman humanism. And inhuman humanism can neither sustain, nor nurture, nor defend the democratic project. It can only undermine it, or attack it.[37]

Getting at the Roots of Things

I wonder, though, if we can't stretch Father de Lubac's analysis backward and forward, chronologically. De Lubac makes a powerful case that communism, fascism, and Nazism were expressions of an atheistic humanism that took its cues from the positivism of Auguste Comte (empirical science is humanity's only reliable tutor), the subjectivism of Feuerbach ("God" is the mythical projection of human aspirations), the materialism of Marx (the spiritual world is an illusion), and the radical willfulness of Nietszche (exercising the will to power is the index of human greatness). But hadn't the rot distorted European civilization earlier than Lenin and Hitler (and their more inept fellow totalitarian, Mussolini)? Perhaps the fullest expression of the material effects of atheistic humanism had to wait until Perm Camp 36 and the killing grounds of the Lubyanka prison, until Treblinka and Sobibor, Maidanek and Auschwitz. But—and here we return to our earlier reflections—doesn't an analysis similar to de Lubac's bring us to a deeper understanding of the civilizational trapgate that was the Great War? Can we explain why Europe fell into Solzhenitsyn's "rage of self-mutilation" without recognizing, as the great Russian writer put it, that men had "forgotten God"? Doesn't de Lubac's suggestion—that this forgetting took place in the name of a false concept of human liberation—help us understand why the forgetting was so powerful and so complete? If we read "history" from beneath the surface of history—if we read history through a theological lens—de Lubac's analysis of the drama of atheistic humanism helps flesh out Solzhenitsyn's identification of 1914–1918 as the moment when European civilization went into crisis.

De Lubac's analysis also sheds light on post–Cold War Europe. For beneath the surface of post–Cold War history we can also find residues of the drama of atheistic humanism. Yes, the most demonic institutional expressions of atheistic humanism were defeated in World War II and the Cold War. But certain intellectual, spiritual, and moral toxins remained. Can we explain Europe's contemporary enthrallment to what the Canadian philosopher Charles Taylor has called exclusive humanism—a humanism determined to exclude transcendent reference points from cultural, social, and political life—without taking full account of the drama of de Lubac's atheistic humanism: without, to repeat, taking account of Comte's positivism, Feuerbach's subjectivism, Marx's materialism, and Nietzsche's will to power? I doubt it. The depoliticization of Europe lamented by Pierre Manent is not the product of the Brussels bureaucracy alone—and neither are the cult of the present and the contempt for tradition decried by Rémi Brague.

Henri de Lubac's penetrating analysis of the drama of atheistic humanism suggests that the "Europe problem" and its analogues in other parts of the West is not simply a twentieth-century problem—although the crisis of European civilizational morale accelerated exponentially during the Great War when, as Pierre Manent writes, "self-sacrifice gave way to self-mutilation and the frenzied love of death."[38] No, the proximate roots of the "Europe problem" that thoughtful Europeans and many Americans experience today go back to the nineteenth century—to the drama of atheistic humanism and the related triumph of secularization, or de-Christianization, in western Europe. For that process of secularization (whose remote origins can be traced back at least as far as the sixteenth-century wars of religion) had profound public consequences: it led to the collapse of a transcendent horizon of moral judgment in European public life and the triumph of what Manent calls the "self-adoration" and "fateful hubris" that led to the Great War and its progeny.[39]

As José Casanova of New York's New School has put it, secularization then became "a self-fulfilling prophecy in Europe. . . a taken-for-granted belief shared not only by sociologists but by a majority of the population."[40] Why European Christianity was particularly vulnerable to the siren song of atheistic humanism raises another, deeper set of questions that are beyond our scope here and that deserve extensive and serious study. Answers to those questions will certainly require carefully probing the Catholic Church's identification with the political forces most resistant to the democratic project in late-eighteen- and nineteenth-century Europe, as well as a more thorough understanding of what democracy meant to those forces that identified the free society with the "laicism" *(laïcité)* that was the precursor to "exclusive humanism." Still, even absent definitive answers to those questions, the proximate cultural roots of today's "Europe problem" can now be identified with some clarity.

European man has convinced himself that in order to be modern and free, he must be radically secular. That conviction has had crucial, indeed lethal, consequences for European public life and European culture. Indeed, that conviction and its public consequences are at the root of Europe's contemporary crisis of civilizational morale. That crisis of civilizational morale, in turn, helps explain why European man is deliberately forgetting his history. That crisis of civilizational morale, in turn, helps us understand why European man is abandoning the hard work and high adventure of democratic politics, seeming to prefer the false domestic security of bureaucracy and the dubious international security offered by the U.N. system. That crisis of civilizational morale is one of the principal reasons why European man is failing to create the human future of Europe.

A Hard Judgment

Writing in the aftermath of World War II, Christopher Dawson took exception to the suggestion that modern European civilization was "pagan." Paganism was rife with religious sentiment, Dawson recalled; what was going on in mid–twentieth century Europe was something different. True, many men and women had ceased to belong to the Church. But rather than belonging to something else, rather than adhering to another community of transcendent allegiance, they now belonged nowhere. This spiritual no-man's-land, as Dawson characterized it, was inherently unstable and ultimately self-destructive. Or, as the usually gentle Dawson put it in an especially fierce passage, "a secular society that has no end beyond its own satisfaction is a monstrosity—a cancerous growth which will ultimately destroy itself."[41] One wonders what Christopher Dawson would say today.

One wonders, in particular, what Christopher Dawson and Henri de Lubac would say about the recent attempt by European intellectuals and European political leaders to airbrush fifteen hundred years of Christian history from Europe's political memory in the process of devising a new constitution for the new Europe—an exercise in self-inflicted amnesia which turns out, on closer examination, to suggest a key to the "Europe problem" and its American parallels.

Growing Body, Withering Soul

On May 1, 2004, ten new members—the Czech Republic, Estonia, the Greek section of Cyprus, Hungary, Latvia, Lithuania, Malta, Poland, Slovakia, and Slovenia—were formally admitted to the European Union, bringing the E.U.'s full membership to twenty-five by joining Austria, Belgium, Denmark, Finland, France, Germany, Great Britain, Greece, Ireland, Italy, Luxembourg, the Netherlands, Portugal, Spain, and Sweden. E.U. expansion, another step toward ending the artificial Cold War division of Europe into "east" and "west," also set in motion a lengthy process of drafting the European Union's first constitution—or, to be technically precise, a European constitutional treaty.

Like all such exercises (including the American one in Philadelphia in 1787), this constitution-making had its share of acrimony and political horse-trading, as old and new members alike struggled to find a method for E.U. decision-making that protected the claims of small states while acknowledging the larger contributions of more populous states to the E.U. coffers; as the relative population size of European countries continues to shift in the decades ahead, this normal process of political adjustment will continue (as indeed it did in the United States as new states entered the union).

At the same time, however, constitution-making set off a fierce controversy that was quite possibly more portentous for Europe's future, although the argument got remarkably little attention in the United States. The question was this: Should the new constitution's preamble make any reference to Christianity in citing the sources of Europe's distinctive civilization? In the draft constitution that formed the basis of the final treaty negotiation in June 2004, the roots of contemporary European civilization and its commitments to democracy, human rights, and the rule of law were identified as the Continent's classical heritage (the draft began with a citation from Thucydides) and the Enlightenment; fifteen hundred years of Christian influence on the formation of what is now Europe went unremarked. The Polish government (largely composed of ex-communists) vigorously protested this omission; so did the Italian government (less vigorously); the governments of the Czech Republic, Lithuania, Malta, and Portugal; and the Spanish government—although Spain's convictions shifted after the government of José Maria Aznar was voted out of office in mid-March 2004.[42] Pope John Paul II, whose support for the European Union was likely decisive in getting a positive vote in Poland during a national referendum on E.U. accession, devoted weeks of Sunday Angelus addresses to the debate in the summer of 2003, arguing sharply at one point that the Christian patrimony of European civilization "cannot be squandered."[43]

In the European public square, however, these were minority voices. In September 2003, President Jacques Chirac of France made his government's position clear: "France is a lay state and as such she does not have a habit of calling for insertions of a religious nature into constitutional texts." The "lay character" of French public institutions, Chirac concluded, would "not allow. . . a religious reference" in the new Euro-constitution.[44] Chirac's *laïcité* was taken a step further by a Socialist member of the French Chamber of Deputies, Olivier Duhamel, who suggested that any mention of God or Christianity in the Euro-constitution would be "absurd," because doing so would exclude Muslims, other non-Christians, and atheists from the political community of the new Europe.[45]

These concerns about exclusion and divisiveness were not French alone. Sweden's *Aftonbladet*, Scandinavia's largest daily, editorialized that any reference to Christian values in the Euro-constitution would be a "huge mistake" because it would "exclude groups and raise new walls."[46] A British Labor member of the European Parliament, Linda McAvan, agreed, saying that any specific mention of Christianity's contributions to European civilization would "offend those many millions of different faiths or no faith at all." Lena Hjelm-Wallen, a former deputy prime minister of Sweden and a member of the European constitutional convention, thought it "a joke" when she heard that Sweden's Christian Democrats wanted the Christian sources of European civilization to be recognized in the constitution's preamble.[47] Former French President Valéry Giscard d'Estaing, who presided over the European constitutional convention, succinctly summed up the case for this side of the debate by noting that "Europeans live in a purely secular political system, where religion does not play an important role."[48]

As a matter of fact, Giscard was mistaken; over half of the E.U. population at the time of the expansion lived in countries that supported established churches or formally acknowledged God in their constitutions. At the same time, however, Giscard and those who shared his opinion about the "purely secular" public life of Europe could point to extraordinarily low levels of Christian practice in contemporary western Europe to buttress their claim that established churches and constitutional nods to God (or, in the case of Ireland, to "the Most Holy Trinity") are vestiges of a past with little relevance to the present—and likely even less impact on the future.

But why was the argument on this question so strident? The ferocity of the opposition to acknowledging any role for Christianity in the formation of today's democratic Europe—the language got quite intemperate when the organized gay and humanist lobbies weighed in—suggests that more was afoot here than a combination of historic French *laïcité*, contemporary European secularity, and a passion for inclusivity. For if the mere mention of a Christian contribution to European civilization "excludes" Jews, Muslims, and nonbelievers, why doesn't the celebration of the Enlightenment "exclude" Aristotelians, Thomists, and indeed postmodernists who think Immanuel Kant and other exponents of Enlightenment rationalism got it wrong? A closer reading of the debate surrounding the preamble leads to the conclusion that, in the minds of many Europeans, Christianity was not simply a non-factor in the development of contemporary European public life; Christianity was (and is) an obstacle to the evolution of a Europe at peace, a Europe that champions human rights, a Europe that governs itself democratically.

It was but a short step from this judgment to the assumption that any mention of Europe's Christian heritage as one part of the foundation on which the future of Europe will be built invites a return to the sixteenth century and a Europe of intolerance, obscurantism, and perhaps even fratricide. *Éscrasez l'infâme*, Voltaire famously advised; crush the [Judeo-Christian] infamy. Judging from the debate in 2003 and 2004 over the preamble to the European constitutional treaty, crushing the "infamy" of Europe's Christian heritage seems, to many contemporary European politicians and intellectuals, a necessary precondition to securing the democratic foundations of an enlarged European Union. A thoroughly secular European public square, in which *laïcité*—now transformed into a modern secularism that is "neutral toward worldviews," as two influential intellectuals, Germany's Jürgen Habermas and France's Jacques Derrida put it—must be the official, pan-European public ideology.[49] A Europe neutral toward worldviews is the only democratic Europe many influential European political leaders and thinkers can imagine. And to take that view of Europe's present and future evidently requires them to argue that nothing of consequence happened between Thucydides (or, perhaps, Marcus Aurelius) and Descartes—at least nothing of consequence for twenty-first-century European democracy and for the defense of human rights.

By the time the draft constitution was completed in June 2004, a grudging reference to "the cultural, religious, and humanist inheritance of Europe" had been shoe-horned into the preamble's first clause (a formulation that a British Foreign Office official described as "so bland as to be meaningless").[50] The draft constitution's Article I-52 also bound the European Union to respect the legal personality and juridical status of churches and other "religious associations" under existing national laws. Still, the preamble agreed on was (as Michelangelo brashly said of Pope Julius II's original plans for the Sistine Chapel ceiling) *una cosa povera*— a poor thing. Moreover, the argument over acknowledging any Christian contribution to the democratic civilization of the twenty-first century spoke volumes about the understandings of "democracy" and "human rights" that shape contemporary European high culture and the political elite in the Brussels-Paris-Berlin axis.

By the time the draft constitution for the expanded European Union was finished and ready to be submitted for ratification by the member states, "Europe" as a political entity resembled nothing so much as a teenager who had just gone through a tremendous physical growth spurt but without a parallel growth in intellectual and moral maturity: physically an adult but spiritually stuck in adolescence.

What Constitutions Do

The most penetrating analysis of the debate over the European constitution and Christianity's place in it, and of what that debate meant both for European constitutionalism and for European democracy, came, not from a European or a Christian, but from an Orthodox Jew, born in South Africa: J. H. H. Weiler, director of the Jean Monnet Center and professor of law at the New York University School of Law. In a small book published in late 2003, *Un'Europa cristiana: Un saggio esplorativo* (Christian Europe: An Exploratory Essay), Weiler, who recognized the historical absurdity of excising Christianity from modern Europe's cultural story, nonetheless chose to challenge Europe's secularists on grounds of legal and political philosophy, arguing that a Euro-constitution that deliberately ignored Europe's Christian roots would be *constitutionally* illegitimate.[51]

Constitutions do three things, Weiler proposed: constitutions organize state functions, identifying the responsibilities and boundaries of the legislature, the executive, and the judiciary; constitutions also define the relationship between citizens and the state. What Europe's secularists seem to have forgotten, Weiler suggests, is the third function of constitution-making and constitutions. Constitutions are the repository, the safe-deposit box, of the values, symbols, and ideas that make a society what it is; constitutions embody what Weiler calls "the *ethos* and the *telos*," the cultural foundations and aspirations, of a given political community. To ignore this third function of constitution-making and constitutions is to jeopardize, even abort, the entire constitutional process, he argued. The Euro-constitution's preamble—its statement of Europe's self-identity— rightly claims that Europe is a continent bearing a distinctive civilization. To deny one of that civilization's "constituting" assets, Weiler insisted, is not simply historically flat-footed. It is *constitutionally* disabling.

On Weiler's argument, therefore, constituting something called Europe without acknowledging its Christian cultural origins is likely to be, at best, an exercise in frustration and, at worst, an exercise in futility. At the same time, Weiler knows that many cultural streams have fed into the making of modern Europe.[52] Thus his understanding of the "Christian Europe" in his book's title is a capacious one:

A "Christian Europe" is not a Europe exclusively or necessarily confessional. It is a Europe that respects equally, in a full and complete way, all its citizens: believers and "laicists," Christians and non-Christians. It is a Europe that, while celebrating the noble heritage of Enlightenment humanism, also abandons its Christophobia and neither fears nor is embarrassed by the recognition that Christianity is one of the central elements in the evolution of its unique civilization. It is, finally, a Europe that, in public discourse about its own past and future, recovers all the riches that can come from confronting one of its two principal intellectual and spiritual traditions: its Christian heritage, particularly [as understood in] the post–Vatican II era by a pope whose teaching makes him second to none in grasping the situation of contemporary history.

What an integrating Europe needs, in other words, is a constitution that protects both "freedom of religion and freedom from religion," as Weiler put it. But adequate constitution-making, Weiler suggests, involves something more than acknowledging that believers and nonbelievers have equal rights in the political community. For Weiler understands that "freedom of religion" would likely be eroded in the future—and perhaps severely—if "freedom from religion," taking the form of historical denial in service to established secularism, were to be imposed on the European public square as part of Europe's constitution-making.

There was another way. After surveying existing European constitutions and their various ways of handling the legitimate rights of both believers and nonbelievers, Weiler proposed that the alternative to a Europe built on the model of the French agnostic state—the imposition of *laïcité* in the name of pluralism, a procedure Weiler dubbed "Orwellian"—could be found in the inclusive solution adopted by Poland in its post–1989 constitution, the preamble to which he cited approvingly:

> Taking care for the existence and the future of our Fatherland, which recovered the possibility of a sovereign and democratic determination of its own destiny in 1989, we, the Polish nation, all the citizens of the

Republic—both those who believe in God as the font of truth, justice, and beauty, and those who do not share this faith but respect these universal values [as they] derive from different fonts—equal in rights and responsibilities with regard to the common good— Poland. . . .

Historical Memory and
Moral Community

The issue of historical memory is not a matter of interest to historians alone. Historical memory, Joseph Weiler insists, is essential for moral community. And there can be no free political community without the foundation of a moral community, a community of shared moral commitments. The draft Euro-constitution recognizes this by celebrating the commitments to freedom, tolerance, and equal civil rights for all that unite Europe today; but the architects of the new Euro-constitution seemed incapable of imagining any role for Christianity in the historical evolution or contemporary defense of those noble commitments. Because of this,

Weiler concludes, Europe's constitutional framers put themselves and their project in a self-contradictory position: imposing an E.U.–enforced *laïcité* on European public life, thereby violating the Euro-constitution's declared moral commitment to "tolerance." The obvious alternative, Weiler concluded, would be a constitution that recognized both the religious and secular "sensibilities" and the contributions each has made to Europe's understanding of human rights and its commitment to democracy. Such a recognition of the truth of history would in turn make it more likely that religiously informed moral argument would have a place in European public life in the future.

During the debate over the European constitution, Joseph Weiler also reminded Europe's contemporary secularists that the founding fathers of today's European Union were all serious Catholics who saw European integration as a project of Christian civilization: Konrad Adenauer, Alcide de Gasperi, Robert Schuman, Jean Monnet. The secularist story of the origins of today's Europe is at best incomplete and misleading, and at worst false and disorienting. And false stories, Weiler suggested, make for defective constitutions. Political commentators, criticizing the elitist character of the process of Europe's constitution-making, had complained for years that the entire project suffered from a "democracy deficit," having been conceived and run by elites with little reference to popular sentiment or will. In the concluding section of his book, Joseph Weiler proposes that the democracy deficit in Europe's constitution-making was in fact a "Christian deficit." For to ignore the Christian roots of European democracy is to ignore the fact that "Christian thought is part of the patrimony of Europe for believers and nonbelievers, Christians and non-Christians, alike."

The various meanings of that patrimony, he acknowledged, are up for robust debate. But to deliberately exclude Europe's Christian heritage from Europe's public life "impoverishes everyone." Connoisseurs of political texts will note that the European constitution approved in June 2004 contains some 70,000 words (almost ten times the length of the U.S. Constitution). Yet the one word that could not be fit into the constitution for the new Europe—"Christianity"—is the embodiment of a story that has arguably had more to do with "constituting" Europe than anything else. What is going on when this story can't be acknowledged? Is it a case, as suggested above, of an adolescent engaging in a typically adolescent rebellion against parents? Is that rebellion in service of a particular (and particularly adolescent) understanding of the freedom that Europe's new constitution is meant to celebrate and advance?

Christophobia

Before getting into that, let's pause for a moment on Joseph Weiler's provocative usage, "Christophobia." When Weiler argues that resistance to any acknowledgment of the Christian sources of Europe's democratic present is a form of Christophobia, what precisely does he mean? He means, in fact, eight things. Taken together, they form an ideological mesh that, in Weiler's judgment, makes it virtually impossible to see, much less acknowledge, the possibility that Christian ideas, Christian ethics, and Christian history have had anything to do with a Europe committed to human rights, democracy, and the rule of law.

The first component of Christophobia is the twentieth-century experience of the Holocaust, and the conviction in European intellectual and political circles that the genocidal depredations of the *Shoah* were the logical outcome of Christian anti-Judaism throughout European history. A Europe saying "Never again!" to Auschwitz and all the rest must therefore say "No" to the possibility that Christianity had anything to do with a tolerant Europe.

The second (and Weiler listed these eight in no particular order of magnitude) is what he calls the "1968 mind-set." The youthful rebellion against traditional authority that made "1968" a more long-lasting phenomenon in Europe than in the United States (which, during the same year, experienced the assassinations of Martin Luther King Jr. and Robert F. Kennedy, vast urban riots, the collapse of the Johnson presidency, and Woodstock) continues today, in one form or another, with the graying veterans of 1968 now well established in European parliaments, cabinets, universities, literary salons, and the media. Part of the rebellion of 1968 was its rebellion against Europe's traditional Christian identity and consciousness. To complete 1968 through the processes of European integration and constitution-making means to complete the erasure of Christianity from any significant place in the European public square.

The third component of Christophobia, Weiler proposes, is formed by a psychological and ideological backlash to the Revolution of 1989 in central and eastern Europe. Here was a nonviolent revolution that did more to expand the zone of democracy in Europe than anything since the defeat of Hitler—and it was deeply, even decisively, influenced by Christianity; preeminently by Pope John Paul II but also by Lutherans in the old East Germany, Christian Czechs of various denominations, Romanian Reformed Christians, and Baptists in Poland and Czechoslovakia, all working with their secular fellow dissidents to overthrow the old order and bring democracy to Stalin's external empire. This, Weiler suggests, was a wrenching experience: a revolution for democracy inspired in no small part by Christians and carried out against the embodiment of hypersecularism in modern politics—communism. The shock to the sensibilities of the people of 1968, many of whom were not exactly stalwarts in the anticommunist cause, was severe. Denial, in the form of this facet of Christophobia, followed, and follows.

The fourth component of contemporary European Christophobia is more overtly political: continuing resentment of the dominant role once played by Christian

Democratic parties in postwar Europe—not only in places like Germany and Italy, where the Christian Democrats were major players electorally, but in the creation of the European Coal and Steel Community, then the Common Market, then the European Community, and so forth. Years in the political wilderness, when the Christian Democrats were riding high, combined with a deliberate forgetfulness about the Christian Democratic inspiration of the European project, have left scars on the European left and among European secularists that form part of their Christophobia today.

Then there is Europe's tendency to parse everything in left/right terms—and then identify Christianity with the right, which is the party (as the left sees it) of xenophobia, racism, intolerance, bigotry, narrowness, nationalism, and everything else Europe must not be.

The sixth source of contemporary European Christophobia, in Joseph Weiler's judgment, is the resentment toward the late Pope John Paul II evident among secularists and Catholic dissidents. The late pope's undeniable role in igniting the revolution of conscience that made possible the Revolution of 1989 in east central Europe, his support for democracy in Latin America and East Asia, his global defense of religious freedom for all, his remarkable reconstruction of Catholic–Jewish relations, his opposition to war and abortion (not to mention his enormous personal authority and his popularity with young people)—all of this was very, very hard to fit into the story line of late modernity or postmodernity as crafted by European secularists and dissenting Catholics. They insisted that John Paul II *must* have been a premodern man, of whom nothing serious could be expected in aid of Europe's democratic future. The alternative possibility—that John Paul II was a thoroughly modern man with an alternative, and perhaps more penetrating, reading of modernity—simply cannot be entertained.

In the seventh place, Christophobia in Europe today is fed by distorted teaching about European history which (as often happens in the United States) stresses the Enlightenment roots of the democratic project to the virtual exclusion of democracy's historic cultural roots in the Christian soil of pre-Enlightenment Europe. Believers as well as nonbelievers have internalized this metanarrative; so it is, perhaps, little wonder that the preamble to the European constitution once proposed to take a giant leap from the Greeks and Romans to Descartes and Kant in describing the historical sources of contemporary European democracy.

Finally, Weiler suggests that the aging children of 1968, now middle-aged and soon to be retired, are upset and confused by the fact that, in some cases, their children have become Christian believers. Those who grew up Christian and rejected both the faith and the Church in late adolescence or early adulthood are puzzled, even angered, by the phenomenon of their children turning to Jesus Christ and Christianity to fill the void in their lives. Having watched this at work in France during Pope John Paul II's World Youth Day in Paris in 1997, when virtually all of *bien-pensant* France was stunned by the massive turnout of young Catholics come to celebrate their newfound faith with their religious hero, I'm inclined to think that on this, as on the other seven points above, Joseph Weiler is on to something. But more on that experience a bit later.

Two Ideas of Freedom

Through the prism of contemporary European intellectual and cultural history, Joseph Weiler helps us
understand why a twenty-first-century European constitution that can accommodate 70,000 other words
found no room for the word "Christianity." Yet I cannot
resist the suspicion that the argument over what became known as the *invocatio Dei* in the European constitution was, in many respects, a stalking horse for
another argument that Europe's constitution makers
really did not want to engage—and that is the argument over the very meaning of freedom. That argument
did not begin with the Enlightenment; it began in the
High Middle Ages and continues to this day. Its origins

are worth revisiting briefly. We can think of it as an argument between two friars.

Thomas Aquinas was born around 1225 in his family *castello* near Roccasecca in the Roman Campagna and died in 1274 at the Abbey of Fossanuova, southeast of Rome. His monumental achievement, in such epic works as the *Summa Contra Gentiles* and the *Summa Theologiae*, was to marry the wisdom of a millennium of Christian philosophy and theology to the "new philosophy" of Aristotle, which Europeans rediscovered in the early thirteenth century. This marriage—which formed a bridge in European culture between the classical world and the medieval world—yielded a rich, complex, and deeply humanistic vision of the human person, human goods, human society, and human destiny. Embedded in that understanding of the human person was a powerful concept of freedom.

According to one of his most eminent contemporary interpreters, the Belgian Dominican Servais Pinckaers, Aquinas's subtle, complex thinking about freedom is best captured in the phrase *freedom for excellence*. Freedom, for Aquinas, is a means to human excellence and human happiness. Freedom is the capacity to choose wisely and act well as a matter of habit—or, to use an old-fashioned term, as a matter of virtue. Freedom, on this understanding, is the means by which we act, through our intelligence and our will, on the natural longing for truth, goodness, and happiness that is built into us as human beings. Freedom grows in us, and the habit of living freedom wisely must be developed through education, which (among many other things) involves the experience of emulating others who live wisely and well. On Thomas's view, freedom is the great organizing principle of the moral life—and because the very possibility of a moral life is what distinguishes human beings from the rest of the natural world, freedom is the great organizing principle of a life lived in a truly human way.

Thus, as Father Pinckaers notes, virtue and the virtues are crucial elements of freedom rightly understood, and the journey of a life lived in freedom is a journey of growth in virtue—growth in our ability to choose wisely and well the things that truly make for our personal happiness and for the common good. It's like playing a musical instrument, Pinckaers suggests—anyone can bang away on a piano, but that's to make noise, not music, and it's a barbaric, not humanistic, expression of freedom. At first, learning to play the piano is a matter of some drudgery, as we master exercises that seem like a constraint, a burden. But as our mastery grows, we discover a new, richer kind of freedom: we can play the music we like, we can create new music on our own. Freedom, in other words, is a matter of gradually acquiring the capacity to choose the good and to do what we choose with perfection, with excellence.

Thus law and freedom are not opposites. Law can educate us in freedom. Law is not something imposed on us externally; rather, law is a work of wisdom, and good law makes it possible for us to achieve the human goods we instinctively seek because of who we are and what we are meant to be as human beings.[53]

This is not a Pollyannaish view of the human condition. Aquinas knew that human beings can and in fact do evil—even great evil. Yet even in the face of manifest evil, Thomas insisted that we have within us, and can develop, a freedom through which we can do things well, rightly, excellently. Evil is not the last word about the human condition, and an awareness of evil is not, as Thomas Hobbes insisted at the beginning of the Enlightenment, the place to begin thinking about freedom or indeed about political life in general. We are made for excellence. Developed through the four cardinal virtues—prudence or practical wisdom, justice, courage, and temperance (perhaps better today, self-mastery)—freedom is the method by which we become the kind of people our noblest instincts incline us to be: the kind of people who can, for example, build free and democratic societies characterized by tolerance, civility, and respect for others, societies in which the rights of all are protected by both law and the moral commitments of "we the people" who make the law.

Our second friar, William of Ockham, was born in England about a dozen years after Thomas Aquinas died, joined the Franciscans, was educated and later taught at Oxford, and died at Munich in 1347 after a life of considerable turbulence. Those who have never studied philosophy will still recognize him as the author of Ockham's razor—the principle (still used in science as well as philosophy) that the simpler of two explanations is, as a general rule, to be preferred. Philosophers consider Ockham the chief exponent of nominalism, a powerful philosophical movement which taught that universal concepts only exist in our minds—they don't exist in reality. Thus, to take an obvious and crucial example, nominalists contend that there is no such thing as "human nature." "Human nature" is simply the description, the name (hence "nominalism"), that we give to our experience of common features among human beings. The only things that exist are particulars.

This trip into the arcana of medieval thinking about thinking (or epistemology) may seem far removed from our concerns about Europe and its constitution-making, but bear with me for just a little longer; the dots will be connected.

Nominalism had a great influence on Christian moral theology. And because politics, as Aristotle proposed, is an extension of ethics, nominalism's impact on moral theology also had a tremendous influence on politics, via political theory. How? Go back to our earlier example. If there is no such thing as human nature, then there are no universal moral principles that can be read from human nature. That means that morality is simply law and obligation, and law is always somewhere outside me. Law, in other words, is always coercion—both divine law and human law, God's coercion of us and our coercion of one another.

Ideas, as always, have consequences. And in these ideas, historian of philosophy Josef Pieper writes, "extremely dangerous processes were being set in motion, and many a future trouble was preparing."[54] Pinckaers, the disciple of Aquinas, writes that Ockham's work was "the first atomic explosion of the modern era." "The atom he split," though, "was. . . not physical but psychic," for Ockham shattered our concept of the world and thereby created a new, atomized vision of the human person and ultimately of society.[55] With Ockham, we meet what Pinckaers calls the *freedom of indifference*.

Here, freedom is simply a neutral faculty of choice. And choice is everything, for choice is a matter of self-assertion, of power. Will is the defining human attribute. Indeed, will is the defining attribute of all reality. For God too is supremely willful, and the moral life, as Ockham understood it, was a contest of wills between my will and God's imposition of His will through, for example, the Ten Commandments.

This radical emphasis on the will was an idea with profound real-world consequences. Willfulness severs human beings from each other in a most dramatic way. For how can there be a "common good" if there are only the particular goods of individual men and women who are acting out their own personal willfulness? So here, in the fourteenth century, is the beginning of what is often called today the autonomy project, whose modern prophet was Nietzsche: the idea that human beings are radically autonomous, self-creating "selves" whose primary relations to one another are relations of power. As Father Pinckaers writes, the freedom of indifference was "impregnated" from the beginning "with a passion for self-affirmation."[56] Thus, over time, freedom was eventually led into the trap of self-interest, from which Immanuel Kant tried unsuccessfully to rescue it by appeals to a categorical imperative that could be known by reason and that would, Kant hoped, restore some objectivity to morality.[57] There were, to be sure, a lot of twists and turns along the way. But it's not a stretch to suggest that William of Ockham was the beginning of the line that eventually led to Nietzsche's will to power and its profound effect on today—not least, through its influence on the civilizational trapgate that was the Great War.

Freedom, for Ockham as for so many European and American intellectuals today, has no spiritual character. The reality is autonomous man, not virtuous man, for freedom has nothing to do with goodness, happiness, or truth. Freedom is simply willfulness. Freedom can attach itself to anything, so long as it doesn't run into a superior will, human or divine. Later in the history of ideas, when God drops out of the picture, freedom as willfulness comes to be understood in purely instrumental or utilitarian terms. And if the road on which Ockham set out eventually leads to Nietzsche, it also leads, through even more twists and turns, to a European constitution that, as Joseph Weiler writes, avoids the questions of both ethics and purpose— of *ethos* and *telos*—because it cannot identify with precision and historical accuracy the sources of Europe's commitments to human rights, democracy, and the rule of law.

If willfulness is all, and freedom is simply the assertion of my "self" (an assertiveness protected by law, so long as "no one else gets hurt"), then it's very diffi-cult, perhaps impossible, to give an account of why that freedom has any value beyond its being an ex-pression of my will. And that seems a very thin foun-dation indeed on which to build a democratic civilization that can sustain itself domestically and de-fend itself in the face of its enemies.

Viewed through the lens of the history of ideas, the argument over the *invocatio Dei* in the European constitution was an argument between the proponents of freedom for excellence and the proponents of the freedom of indifference. A medieval debate between two friars played itself out in twenty-first-century constitution-making. The freedom of indifference seems to have won, for the moment. The conse-quences are likely to be considerable.

By Name

Enough of philosophy for the moment. Think briefly about the following larger-than-life personalities—saints and warriors, artists and musicians, authors and intellectuals, politicians and mystics:

Adalbert (Wojciech): apostle of the Poles.

Konrad Adenauer: German chancellor, co-founder of the European Union.

Albert the Great: philosopher, scientist, theologian.

Ambrose of Milan: theologian.

Fra Angelico: painter.

Anskar: apostle of Scandinavia.

Thomas Aquinas: philosopher and theologian.

Athanasius: theologian.

Augustine of Canterbury: apostle of the English.

Augustine of Hippo: theologian.

Johann Sebastian Bach: composer.

Roger Bacon: scientist and encyclopedist.

Thomas Becket: opponent of royal absolutism, defender of the liberty of the Church.

Bede: proto-historian of England.

Belisarius: Byzantine general.

Benedict: founder of western monasticism, preserver of civilization.

Bernard of Clairvaux: preacher and theologian.

Gianlorenzo Bernini: sculptor, architect.

Dietrich Bonhoeffer: theologian, opponent of Nazi absolutism.

Boniface: apostle of the Germans.

Charles Borromeo: theologian and reformer of the Catholic Church.

Hieronymus Bosch: painter.

Bridget of Sweden: queen and religious foundress.

John Calvin: theologian.

Caravaggio: painter.

Charlemagne: emperor.

El Cid (Rodrigo Diáz): knight and legend.

Clovis: king.

Christopher Columbus: explorer.

Constantine: emperor.

Oliver Cromwell: soldier and statesman.

Cyril and Methodius: apostles of the Slavs, linguists.

Dante: poet.

Dominic: religious founder.

Don John: soldier, defender of Europe in 1571.

Fyodor Dostoevsky: novelist.

Edward the Confessor: king.

Elizabeth I: queen.

Erasmus of Rotterdam: humanist.

Gabriel Fauré: composer.

Ferdinand of Aragon and Isabella of Castile: defenders of Europe in 1492.

Francis of Assisi: religious founder, poet, and mystic.

Galileo Galilei: scientist.

Alcide de Gasperi: Italian prime minister, co-founder of the European Union.

Gregory the Great: pope, theologian, defender of civilization.

Gregory VII: pope and defender of the Church's liberty.

Gustavus Adolphus: king.

Johann Gutenberg: inventor, printer.

Henry the Navigator: explorer.

Hildegard of Bingen: mystic.

Jan Hus: theologian.

Ignatius of Loyola: religious founder.

Innocent III: pope and protector of mendicants.

Władysław Jagiełło and Jadwiga: founders of the Polish-Lithuanian Commonwealth.

Joachim of Fiore: mystic.

Joan of Arc: soldier and defender of France.

Juan Carlos and Sophia: king and queen of Spain, defenders of democracy.

Bartolomé de Las Casas: defender of universal human rights.

Leo the Great: pope, theologian, defender of civilization.

Louis IX: king and crusader.

Martin Luther: theologian and translator.

Jacques Maritain: philosopher.

Charles Martel: king and defender of Europe in 732.

Gregor Mendel: monk, geneticist.

Michelangelo: sculptor, painter, architect.

Mieszko I: Polish prince and convert.

John Milton: poet.

Jean Monnet: diplomat, co-founder of the European Union.

Thomas More: humanist and statesman.

Wolfgang Amadeus Mozart: composer.

Odo: monastic reformer.

Giovanni Pierluigi da Palestrina: composer.

Patrick: apostle of Ireland.

Charles Péguy: poet.

Peter and Paul: apostles of Europe.

"Prester John": legend.

Raffaelo: painter.

Georges Rouault: painter.

Andrei Rublev: iconographer.

Scholastica: religious foundress.

Robert Schuman: French foreign minister, co-founder of the European Union.

Jan III Sobieski: Polish king, defender of Europe in 1683.

Bernadette Soubirous: visionary of Lourdes.

Stanisław: opponent of royal absolution and defender of the liberty of the Church.

Stephen of Hungary: king.

Wit Stwosz: wood-carver.

Teresa of Ávila: mystic, theologian, memoirist.

Volodymyr: prince of Kievan Rus' and convert.

Lech Wałęsa: non-violent revolutionary.

John Wesley: preacher and social reformer.

William Wilberforce: parliamentary opponent of slavery.

Paweł Włodkovic: humanist, proponent of religious freedom.

John Wycliffe: biblical scholar.

Stefan Wyszyński: opponent of communist absolutism, defender of the liberty of the Church.

Huldrich Zwingli: theologian.

Is it possible to imagine something called "Europe" without men and women such as these—all of them motivated in their life's work, however glorious and however ambiguous, by Christian conviction?

Is it possible to imagine a Europe cherishing "the universal values of the inviolable and inalienable rights of the human person" (as the preamble to the European constitution put it) if these men and women, and the lives and history they shaped, had never existed?

Is it possible to conceive Europe as "a special area of human hope" (another phrase from the preamble) without the witness of these makers of Europe?

And is it possible to imagine a future dedicated to those universal values, a future in which Europe maintains itself as a continent of hope, if Europe cuts itself off from the heritage represented by these figures?

It seems very unlikely.

Making Europe "Europe"

Joseph Weiler argues that the secularist account of the origins of today's Europe is at best incomplete, a repudiation of "part of the patrimony of Europe for believers and nonbelievers, Christians and non-Christians, alike." The complex meaning of that patrimony is certainly a subject for legitimate debate. But to deny it, Weiler suggests, is to play false to Europe's story and to democracy itself.

How, then, did Christianity help "make" Europe?

Princeton's Peter Brown helps us understand that story in his monumental study, *The Rise of Western Christendom: Triumph and Diversity, A.D. 200–1000.*[58] One particular image from *The Rise of Western*

Christendom was permanently fixed in my mind
through five hundred pages of a narrative that ebbed
and flowed between the grand sweep and the poignant
detail: two boys living several thousand miles apart,
about 700 A.D., one in what is now County Antrim, Ireland, the other in Panjikent, east of Samarkand in Central Asia. The boys are doing their lessons in
copybooks. The former writes in Latin, in wax on
wood, the latter in Syriac, on potsherds. Both are in-
dustriously copying the Psalms. As Brown nicely puts
it, "In both milieux, something very similar was happening. Schoolboys, whose native languages were Irish
in Antrim and Soghdian in Panjikent, tried to make
their own, by this laborious method, the Latin and Syriac versions, respectively, of what had become a truly
international sacred text—the 'Holy Scriptures' of the
Christians."[59]

How account for this remarkable synchronicity of
experience? One familiar answer was sketched by
Christopher Dawson, the mid–twentieth century English Catholic convert and (in his own terms) "metahis-
torian," whom we have already met. According to
Dawson's metanarrative of Europe, Rome was the center of a civilizational enterprise that extended from the
British Isles through North Africa and on to the Syriac-
speaking worlds of the Middle East and Central Asia.

When Rome's defensive perimeter collapsed, that civilizational enterprise was shattered by my ancestors, conventionally known as the barbarians. What remained of Roman civilization was preserved by monks in the so-called Dark Ages. These monks later sallied forth from their cloisters to convert the barbarian hordes. Their greatest success was with the Franks, who subsequently produced Charlemagne, whose Carolingian empire preserved the achievements of Roman civilization and set the foundations for what we now call Europe.

Told in these terms, the high point of the story comes on Christmas in the year 800, when Charlemagne was crowned Holy Roman Emperor by Pope Leo III (an event marked to this day by the large red porphyry disk on which Charlemagne knelt, which is lodged in the marble floor of the nave of St. Peter's basilica in Rome). In Charlemagne and Leo III, Rome embraced the "barbarians" and they embraced Rome (and, by extension, Athens and Jerusalem); the civilization we call Europe was thus poised on the cusp of its first great moment of flourishing, the Middle Ages.

Like Christopher Dawson before him, Peter Brown knows that there is no understanding Europe without Christianity. But forty years of scholarship, his own and others, have persuaded him that Dawson's story line—

expansion (the Roman Empire), contraction (barbarian invasions and Dark Ages), absorption (Charlemagne)—is too simple. My ancestors were not, Brown insists, those familiar "Wagnerian figures, with winged helmets, scale-mail breastplates, cloaks trimmed with fur, and baggy trousers."[60] Rather, they were rural people who interacted commercially and socially with Romans along a wide and relatively permeable border that ran straight across what we now call Europe, following the Rhine and the Danube. It was a far more diverse business than Dawson's account allows. Thus it's best, Brown argues, to abandon Dawson's image of a Roman center which, after a Dark Age of contraction, eventually reaches out to include the barbarians of the periphery in a civilizing synthesis that produces Europe. There was no such center, in Brown's view—at least in the terms that Dawson, for whom the center was the Roman Empire and its successor, the Catholic Church, understood it.

On the other hand, Peter Brown is too sophisticated a historian to miss the obvious—that there *was* a kind of center, one that accounted for the triumph and one that disciplined the diversity of his book's subtitle. That center was Christianity, or what Brown calls the "interconnectivity" of Christianity—and it was exemplified in our two eighth-century schoolboys and their copy-books. One was growing up in what would become western Christendom, the other in the Christian east. Both, however, were part of an interconnected civilizational enterprise that stretched from the west coast of Ireland to the steppes of Asia—no matter how much their Catholic and Orthodox descendants would deny that after the mutual excommunications of 1054 A.D., and no matter how much ideologically hardened European secularists deny it today. Western Christendom, for its part, was the product of the complex, diverse encounter between the barbarians and a remarkably flexible Christianity that, for all its adaptability, lived within established doctrinal boundaries.

All of which makes for a richer narrative than conventional expansion-contraction-absorption accounts; both Christianity and "the barbarians" were changed in the process, as some of the great names cited above remind us: Gregory the Great, Augustine of Canterbury, Patrick (author of "the first pieces of extensive Latin prose to be written from beyond the frontiers of the Roman world"),[61] Bede, and Boniface. At the same time, it was what historian Robert Louis Wilken calls the "solidity" of Christianity that made its flexibility possible and gave rise, in the centuries immediately following Brown's narrative, to the distinctive Christian civilization of the High Middle Ages.[62]

Which was, of course, the European civilization which produced the cathedral that stands in contrast to the modernist cube of La Grande Arche.

Those Not-So-Benighted Middle Ages

Anglo-Americans are often taught that the roots of modern democracy can be found in the Glorious Revolution of 1688, which secured parliamentary supremacy against royal absolutism in what would become Great Britain. Continental Europe often imagines democracy beginning in 1789, with the French Revolution. The remarkable civilizational story told by Christopher Dawson and Peter Brown suggests, however, that these readings are myopic, nearsighted. For the way that the Christian civilization of the Middle Ages settled certain struggles between the Catholic Church and the public authorities of the day taught "Europe" lessons that would later be applied to the defense of what we call "human rights" and to the democratic project.

Within seventy-five years of the end of Peter Brown's story, Pope Gregory VII (1073–1085) was embroiled in the investiture controversy, which had to do with whether the pope or the emperor would nominate and "invest" bishops—the heads of local churches. It was a theological and legal argument fraught with historic consequences. The Holy Roman Emperor, Henry IV, knelt in the snow at Canossa, doing penance before Gregory VII; Henry later drove Gregory out of Rome and into exile in Salerno, where he died; the controversy continued. But when the political and ecclesiastical dust finally settled, European civilization had learned some things from the struggle between pope and emperor—or, to indulge in an anachronism, between Church and state.

Had the emperors succeeded in making the Church an administrative/spiritual subdivision of the empire, more would have been lost than the *libertas ecclesiae*, the capacity of the Church to order its own internal life. The possibility of institutional pluralism in the West might have been lost or, at the very least, delayed. Pope Gregory VII defended the Church's prerogative to decide who would become part of the apostolic succession of bishops. At the same time, the effect of his successful defense of the Church's rights was to accelerate social diversity and institutional pluralism in Europe and thus lay the sociological foundations for what contemporary Europeans and Americans call civil society.[63]

Thanks to the resolution of the investiture controversy in favor of the Church, the state (to indulge that anachronism again) would not be all in all. The state would not occupy every inch of social space. Indeed, the state had to acknowledge that there were some things it couldn't do because it was simply incompetent to do them—and that acknowledgment of limited competence created the social and cultural conditions for the possibility of what a later generation of constitutionalists and democrats called the limited state. The Western ideal—a limited state in a free society—was made possible in no small part by the investiture controversy.

The experience of the Christian east highlights how important this development was in the Christian west. Byzantine Christianity's ideal was a "symphony" or "harmony" of emperor and Church—but in practice, that usually meant the subordination of the patriarch of Constantinople to the Byzantine emperor, a subordination that lasted until the collapse of Byzantium in 1453.

Royal absolutism in the west was an aberration. Czarist absolutism in Russia, where Moscow imagined itself the successor to Constantinople as the Third Rome, was a logical extension of the patterns of relationship between Church and state, and the consequent deficit in social and institutional pluralism that had long characterized Byzantine Christianity. Is it any wonder that the Orthodox churches have had such a difficult time adjusting to life after absolutism (meaning, in our time, life after communism) in Russia and other former component parts of the Soviet Union and its external empire? Is it any wonder that democratic transitions have been more difficult in those same lands than in lands whose culture was formed by western Christianity?

Democracy is not simply a matter of procedures; democracy is a matter of ideas, ideals, and moral commitments. What else of consequence for democracy did the Christian civilization of the Middle Ages teach western Europe?

In the first instance, Christianity taught European man his own dignity. Christianity taught an emerging Europe a proper respect for individuality (in sharp contrast to Islam, for example). The Christian idea of vocation—the unique role that each Christian plays in the cosmic drama of creation and redemption—is one root of the Western idea of individualism, which was not, in its origins, a matter of self-constituting autonomy but of living out the singular, God-given destiny that is every human life. Moreover, the Christian doctrines of the Incarnation (God entering history in the flesh) and the Redemption ("God so loved the world that he gave his only Son. . . not to condemn the world, but that the world might be saved through him" [John 3:16–17]) gave the world a dignity it could not achieve by its own efforts. Worldliness, in the Christian sense of the term, can have a noble meaning: the core Western conviction about history—that the human story is not just one damn thing after another—was deeply influenced by Christian doctrine.

That is why, according to Canadian commentator David Warren, it is possible "to speak without self-contradiction of Christian humanism . . . and why it is an error to conceive of the Enlightenment and all that followed it as a complete breach from Christian history." The Enlightenment's commitment to the claims of reason, Warren continues, "owe[s] even more to Thomas Aquinas than to Voltaire; its spiritual flavor is discernible in Augustine. Even the ideas that exploded in the Paris of 1789 were present in the Paris of 1277." Christianity could give birth to the humanism of the

Renaissance and later could engage the Enlightenment because, as Warren concludes, "these things were implicit in it."[64]

As we've seen, the fact of the Church and its claims to authority over men's lives meant that the emperor (later the state) could not be all in all. Politics was thereby desacralized: because God was God, Caesar was not God and neither were Caesar's successors, be they kings, princes, prime ministers, presidents . . . or members of the Politburo. Because Caesar was not God, the "reach" of public authorities was understood to be circumscribed (at least in principle), the cultural ground on which a politics of consent could be built was prepared, and an antitotalitarian vaccine was injected into Europe's civilizational bloodstream. By the same token, it was in the school of Christian culture that Europe learned about the proper dignity of the secular: according to the Church, which took this teaching from its Jewish parent, the human task was to humanize the world, which in Christian terms meant learning to be "at home" in the world even as one prepared for the world to come. Thus Christianity taught Europe that the human task was to enable the world to realize its possibilities. This commitment, the Christian understanding of natural law (nature has its own integrity and rationality), and medieval scholasticism's rigorous logic helped prepare the cultural ground for the rise of modern science. (When Einstein observed that God does not play dice, he was expressing a Judeo-Christian intuition.)[65]

Europe also learned from Christianity that a transcendent order of justice stood in judgment on public authority and its power: what was right wasn't simply what the people in political power declared to be right. If what was right in the ordering of public life could be learned by thinking seriously about what Mr. Jefferson would have called "the laws of nature, and of nature's God," then, in principle, everyone had a claim to an opinion, worthy to be heard, about what justice required in a given circumstance. The rule of law (as distinguished from the rule of divine-right monarchs) and the principle of consent in governance find their deepest roots, not in Enlightenment political theorizing but in ideas, ideals, and moral commitments first nurtured in European Christian culture.

It takes a deliberate act of willfulness—an act of Christophobia, to borrow from Joseph Weiler—to dismiss the notion that this rich civilizational soil contains the nutrients that nourished the democratic possibility in Europe and throughout the Western world. The

Whig theory of history has it wrong, and so do the French; or, at the very least the Whig and French theories of the origins of democracy are woefully incomplete. The democratic project did not emerge, a kind of political virgin birth, in either the Glorious Revolution of 1688 or the 1789 Declaration of the Rights of Man and Citizen. To be sure, those were crucial turning points in the history of modern political thought and in democratic political institutions. But the cultural foundations for the ideas and institutions of self-governance had been laid centuries before in the European universities (entirely Christian in their origins); in such Christian practices as the direct, democratic election of superiors in Benedictine monasteries; in the pilgrimage tradition by which the men and women of an emerging Europe met and came to understand themselves as members of a common civilizational enterprise; in the rich social pluralism of medieval life; and in the cultural instincts and commitments that were gleaned from these distinctively European experiences.[66] (Indeed, there could be no writing of the history of the peoples of Europe absent what historian Norman Davies calls the "natural gateway" of parish registers, for parishes long antedated civil administrative units in Europe.)[67] In that sense, Peter Brown and Christopher

Dawson, who would have disagreed on precisely how it happened, are agreed on the more fundamental point: there is no understanding "Europe" without taking the full measure of what Christianity taught European man about himself, his dignity, his destiny, and his communities—including his political communities.[68]

Giving an Account

If democracy is more than institutions and procedures—if democratic institutions and procedures are
the expressions of a distinctive way of life based on
specific moral commitments—then democratic citizenship must be more than a matter of following the procedures and abiding by the laws and regulations agreed
on by the institutions. A democratic citizen is someone
who can give an account of his or her commitment to
human rights, to the ordered conversation about public
goods that is pluralism, to the rule of law and equality
before the law, to decision-making by the majority and
protection of the rights of minorities. Democratic citizenship means being able to tell *why* one affirms "the

universal values of the inviolable and inalienable rights of the human person, democracy, equality, freedom and the rule of law," to cite the preamble to the European constitution again. Being able to tell *why* those are good things to be preserved, enriched, and defended is essential to everything else to which the constitution commits Europe: "progress and prosperity, for the good of all . . . including the weakest and most deprived . . . [openness] to culture, learning, and social progress . . . peace, justice, and solidarity throughout the world."

Who can give such an account—especially in times when tolerance becomes difficult and civility risks becoming frayed?

There are many ironies involved in the question of the cube and the cathedral; here is one of the richest. The original charge against Christians in the Roman Empire was that they were atheists: people who were *a-theos*, people who had abandoned the gods of Rome and were accountable to another God—and who were thus a threat to public life and public order. To be *a-theos* was to stand outside the political community; indeed, it was to stand over against the political community. The Christophobia of contemporary European high culture turns this indictment inside out and upside down: Christianity cannot be acknowledged as one of the primary sources of European democracy because the only public space safe for pluralism, tolerance, civility, and democracy is, on this telling, a public space that is thoroughly *a-theos*. It is all very strange.[69]

For the truth of the matter is that European Christians can likely give a thicker, more compelling account of their commitment to the values of democracy than their fellow Europeans who are *a-theos*—who believe that "neutrality toward worldviews" must characterize democratic Europe. That, in any case, is Joseph Weiler's view. Tolerance, he argues, is a civic discipline, not just a personal attitude or a cast of mind. A postmodern or neo-Kantian neutrality toward worldviews cannot be truly tolerant, he suggests; it can only be indifferent. Absent convictions, there is no tolerance; there is only indifference. Absent some compelling notion of the truth that requires us to be tolerant of those who have a different understanding of the truth of things, there is only skepticism and relativism.

And skepticism and relativism would seem to be weak foundations on which to build and sustain a pluralistic democracy, for neither skepticism nor relativism, by their own logic, can "give an account" of why Europeans should be tolerant and civil. Why not? Because skepticism and relativism bespeak people who are, quite self-consciously, *a-theos*—for whom the only humanism is ultramundane humanism.

In contrast to this thin account of tolerance—we should be tolerant because it works better, the tolerance of indifference being less messy than the true tolerance of differences engaged civilly—Weiler proposes the argument for tolerance given by Pope John Paul II in his 1989 encyclical letter on Christian mission, *Redemptoris Missio* (The Mission of the Redeemer). In that encyclical, the Pope taught that *"The Church proposes; she imposes nothing."*[70] The Catholic Church respects the Other as an Other who is also a seeker of truth and goodness; the Church asks that the believer and the Other enter into a conversation, a dialogue that leads to mutual enrichment rather than to a deeper skepticism about the very possibility of grasping the truth of things.

Thus the Catholic Church, tutored by the Second Vatican Council and John Paul II, can give an account of its commitment to tolerance, because the Catholic Church believes it to be the will of God that Christians be tolerant of those who have a different view of God's will, or no view of God's will; the Church only asks that it be permitted to enter into conversation with those Others. The Catholic Church, Weiler concludes, has a "conceptual architecture" in which tolerance makes sense—a way of thinking about tolerance that can defend tolerance in times of conflict, when tolerance becomes hard and can even seem threatening. Christians can "give an account" of their defense of the Other's freedom, even if the Other, skeptical and relativist, finds it hard to give an account of the freedom of the Christian.

The Church's account of its commitment to tolerance, dialogue, and the method of persuasion is based on the weightiest of reasons: God requires this of Christians. As the Congregation for the Doctrine of the Faith, the Catholic Church's doctrinal agency, put it in its *Instruction on Christian Freedom and Liberation* (1986), "God wishes to be adored by people who are free."[71] That is why the Church opposed the evil of totalitarianism: it violated the radical freedom of human beings before the mystery of God. Totalitarianism coerced consciences. Only the method of dialogue and persuasion can invite the act of faith, which must be a free act in order to be a humanly authentic act.

That the Church did not always behave according to these convictions is obvious from history, especially European history. Church-sanctioned state persecution of heretics, or the coerced conversion of Spanish Jews that produced the Marranos (Jews who formally converted to

Catholicism in order to remain in Spain after the expulsions of 1492 but remained Jewish in their convictions and private practice), are facts of history—even if the black legend that surrounds these and similar events in the European settlement of the Americas is frequently exaggerated. The point today is that the Church recognizes publicly that these acts of coercion were offenses against its own true doctrine. That is why, on the First Sunday of Lent, March 12, 2000, Pope John Paul II led a Day of Pardon at St. Peter's Basilica. During the solemn Mass, Cardinal Joseph Ratzinger asked God's pardon for the times when Christians "used methods not in keeping with the Gospel in the solemn duty of defending the truth," and then Archbishop (later Cardinal) Francis Xavier Nguyên Van Thuân (a former political prisoner in Vietnam) asked God's forgiveness for the sins Christians had committed against human rights. This was not an exercise in Catholic political correctness, on the model of President Bill Clinton's "apology" for slavery, nor was this pandering to approved victim groups. This was a solemn act of repentance, addressed to the Church's Lord, asking *God's* forgiveness for Christian failures to live the truth of Christian convictions about the dignity of the human person. This was, in a word, confession: an acknowledgment of sin and a plea for divine mercy. As such, it recommitted the Church to live out the truth it professed about the freedom of the human person to seek the truth and adhere to it.[72]

A community capable of such acts—the community of the cathedral, if you will—is a community capable of coming to grips with the shadow side of its history, capable of learning from the past, capable of a reformed life. A community capable of such acts of public repentance is a community that can give a compelling account of its commitments to freedom.

Can others? Can those who are *a-theos*—can the people of the cube—grapple with the dark passages in European history caused by radically secularist understandings of the human person, human community, and human destiny: the depredations of the French Reign of Terror, Nazism, and communism?

What False Stories Do

Let's remain for a moment with the late Pope John Paul II. It's hard to imagine a more thoroughly European figure in recent history. He spoke the languages of Europe, east and west, fluently. He has read widely and deeply in European literature and philosophy; he may have been one of the only men in the world who read contemporary European philosophies of dialogue and hermeneutics for pleasure. His life experience spanned the contemporary history of Europe—the springtime of nations that followed World War I; the darkening shadow of totalitarianism; the Second World War and the Holocaust, in which he lost personal friends; the Nazi attempt to enslave his fellow Poles as *Untermenschen*;

the betrayal of the promise of postwar freedom at the Tehran and Yalta conferences, as well as the subsequent division of Europe into east and west; the depredations of Stalinism and the dangers of the Cold War; the communist crack-up and the rebirth of freedom east of the Elbe River; the end of divided Europe and the revival of a Europe capable, as he put it many times, of "breathing with both lungs." He traveled to virtually every corner of Europe; by late 2004, John Paul had made nine pilgrimages to Iberia, two to the British Isles, one to Scandinavia, one to Finland, eight to Poland, eighteen to the other new democracies of east central and southern Europe, three to the Baltic republics, one to Greece, three to Malta, three to Germany, one to Ukraine, three to Switzerland, four to the Benelux countries, and seven to France, not counting dozens of such trips within Italy.

Moreover, even thoroughly secular readers of contemporary European history acknowledge that John Paul II was far more than an observer of his times. In the case of the Revolution of 1989, he was an active and influential participant; as even Mikhail Gorbachev, last leader of the late Soviet Union, concedes, the revolution of conscience the late pope ignited in Poland and throughout east central Europe in the late 1970s and early 1980s was a crucial factor in the nonviolent political revolution that brought down the Wall and reunited

Europe after forty-five years. Absent John Paul II, there might not be an argument about the future of a re-united "Europe" today.

What John Paul had to say about the future of Europe deserves everyone's attention. If anyone's experience gave him a claim to be heard, it was Karol Wojtyła of Kraków and Rome.

Ten years after the Wall came down, in October 1999, the Catholic bishops of Europe met in Rome in a continental Synod organized around the theme, "That we may be witnesses of Christ who has set us free." Their month-long deliberations were synthesized in an "apostolic exhortation" written by John Paul II and is-sued on June 28, 2003. The exhortation, entitled *Ecclesia in Europa* (The Church in Europe), proposed that the Church of the twenty-first century must once again "proclaim . . . [a] message of hope to a Europe that seems to have lost sight of it."[73]

The bishops, as well as John Paul, were painfully aware of what *Ecclesia in Europa* described as "grave uncertainties at the levels of culture, anthropology, ethics, and spirituality."[74] Europe ought to have experienced a new burst of hope and confidence after seventy-seven years of turmoil; yet what it seemed to be living was an experience of ambiguity that had led to a loss of faith in the future. Thus Europe's most urgent need was not for a common currency, a transnational parliament, a unified set of fiscal and budgetary norms, or a Continent-wide regulatory regime. No, "the most urgent matter Europe faces, in both East and West, is a growing need for hope, a hope which will enable us to give meaning to life and history and to continue on our way together."[75]

The manifestations of this loss of hope were not difficult to identify:

- "A kind of practical agnosticism and religious indifference whereby many Europeans give the impression of living without spiritual roots and somewhat like heirs who have squandered a patrimony entrusted to them by history"

- "Fear of the future"

- "Inner emptiness that grips many people"

- "Widespread existential fragmentation" in which "a feeling of loneliness is prevalent"

- "Weakening of the very concept of the family"

- "Selfishness that closes individuals and groups in upon themselves"

- "A growing lack of concern for ethics and an obsessive concern for personal interests and privileges" leading to "the diminished number of births."[76]

Thus it came as "no real surprise . . . that there are efforts to create a vision of Europe which ignores its religious heritage, and in particular, its profound Christian soul. . . ." These efforts compounded, rather than resolved, the problem of Europe's hope for the future, however, because they misdiagnosed the malady— which was, to return to Henri de Lubac, a by-product of the drama of atheistic humanism: "At the root of this loss of hope is an attempt to promote a vision of man apart from God and apart from Christ. . . . Forgetfulness of God [has] led to the abandonment of man."[77] And that abandonment left European men and women alone in a profoundly, existentially painful way: "One of the roots of the hopelessness that assails many people today is . . . their inability to see themselves as sinners and to allow themselves to be forgiven, an inability often resulting from the isolation of those who, by living as if God did not exist, have no one from whom they can seek forgiveness."[78]

Yet it would be just as false, John Paul II wrote, to suggest that the shadows over Europe were the sum total of the European reality. The Christian martyrs under Nazism and communism demonstrated with their lives their commitment to the gospel of Christ, which had the capacity to build a "moral and societal life which honors and promotes the dignity and freedom of

every person." Freedom's triumph in the formerly communist world, the reincorporation of the countries of the
old Warsaw Pact into Europe, reconciliation between
countries that had been the cockpit of conflict for centuries, the commitment to democracy in governance and
to negotiation as a method of intra-European conflict
resolution, the rise of a genuinely "European consciousness," a widespread if often confused "desire for spiritual nourishment"—all of these new realities of recent
and contemporary European life, important in themselves, also suggested the possibility of a recovery of
"ethical and spiritual values" in "creative fidelity to the
humanist and Christian traditions of our continent."[79]

John Paul II also insisted that the story of Europe
not be told exclusively through the prism of 1789, much
less 1968. For it was from "the biblical conception of
man [that] Europe drew the best of its humanistic culture, found inspiration for its artistic and intellectual
creations, created systems of law and, not least, advanced the dignity of the person as the subject of inalienable rights."[80] Moreover, the late pope argued, it
was this patrimony that had given Europe its uniquely
creative role in world history: "The Church, as the
bearer of the Gospel, thus helped to spread and consoli-
date those values which have made European culture
universal."[81] In an echo of G. K. Chesterton's observa-

tion that modernity's problem was one of "virtues gone mad," John Paul suggested that when "the great values which amply inspired European culture" are willfully "separated from the Gospel," those virtues (e.g., tolerance and civility) "[lose] their very soul and [pave] the way for any number of aberrations:" for example, enforcing *laïcité* in the name of tolerance and pluralism.[82]

If Europe was experiencing hopelessness—and if one result of that hopelessness was a form of demographic suicide—then Europe was dying from a false story, John Paul seemed to be suggesting. Recovering the true story of the sources of European civilization was more than a matter of historical truth-telling. It was the remedy for what ailed Europe at the onset of a new century and millennium.

A Free and Virtuous Europe

It is not the Church's business to run Europe or European states; the days of altar and throne are long since past, and John Paul's *Ecclesia in Europe* betrayed not the slightest nostalgia for the world of the ancien régime. What the Church has to offer the new Europe of the twenty-first century is far more important than what it offered the world of European high politics in the days when Cardinal Wolsey was Lord Chancellor of England, when Cardinal Mazarin was tutor to the future Louis XIV of France, and when Cardinal Consalvi, secretary of state to Pope Pius VII, sat as a peer among equals at the Congress of Vienna, redesigning post-Napoleonic Europe. What the Church proposes to

Europe today is a challenge: a challenge to "the moral quality of its civilization." Absent a secure and publicly assertive moral culture, the machines of democracy and the free economy cannot run well over the long haul; a moral culture capable of disciplining and directing the tremendous energies set loose by free politics and free economics is an essential third component of the architecture of the free society. Catholic social doctrine, based on principles of natural law and proposing a vision of the free *and virtuous* society, can be engaged by every European; it offers an ecumenical and interreligious grammar capable of creating a genuine conversation that engages believers and nonbelievers alike, out of the cacophony that too often passes for European public discourse today. The Church's social doctrine thus offers Europe the possibility of defending the "moral structure of freedom, so as to protect European culture and society both from the totalitarian utopia of 'justice without freedom' and from the utopia of 'freedom without truth' which goes hand in hand with a false concept of 'tolerance.'" Both these utopias, John Paul II reminded his readers, "portend errors and horrors for humanity, as the recent history of Europe sadly attests."[83]

In contrast to the "thin" concept of Europe that would ultimately shape the (ironically thick) European constitution, John Paul II proposed a richer vision: Europe was not, and could not be, merely a geographical area stitched together by the profession of certain values whose primary claim to allegiance is that they work. No, Europe was and is "primarily a cultural and historical concept" in which Christianity had been, and would be, indispensable in creating a society "capable of integrating peoples and cultures among themselves" in a "new model of unity in diversity." The new European Union "will lack substance if it is reduced to its merely geographic and economic dimensions," John Paul cautioned. On the contrary:

> Europe needs a religious dimension. If it is to be "new," by analogy with what is said about the "new city" of the Book of Revelation [cf. 21.2], it must open itself to the workings of God. The hope of building a more just world, a world more worthy of man, cannot prescind from a realization that human effort will be of no avail unless it is accompanied by divine assistance: for "unless the Lord builds the house, those who build it labor in vain" [Psalm 27.1]. For Europe to be built on solid foundations, there is a need to call upon authentic values grounded in the universal moral law written on the heart of every man and woman.[84]

Typically, John Paul closed *Ecclesia in Europa* by calling his fellow Europeans to courage and hope: "Do not be afraid! The Gospel is not against you, but for you. . . . The Gospel of hope does not disappoint! Throughout the vicissitudes of your history, yesterday and today, it is the light which illumines and directs your way; it is the strength which sustains you in trials; it is the prophecy of a new world; it is the sign of a new beginning; it is the invitation to everyone, believers and non-believers alike, to blaze new trails leading to a 'Europe of the spirit,' in order to make the continent a true 'common home' filled with the joy of life."[85]

It is a powerful, compelling, even moving vision that ought to stir the emotions of everyone, European and American, who cares about Europe. At the same time, the Pope's choice of the book of Revelation as the biblical "framework" for *Ecclesia in Europa* was suggestive—even cautionary. The book of Revelation is addressed to the seven churches of Asia Minor in the first century A.D. Few of those churches exist as living Christian communities today, and the classical European civilization of which they were a product was erased by the rising tide of Islam. Europe is not guaranteed a future, John Paul II seemed to be suggesting by his choice of texts from Revelation. Europe must choose the future.

And choosing the future requires, among many other things, reclaiming the Christian spiritual and moral patrimony that helps make Europe "Europe."

Choosing the future means confronting, honestly, the relationship between the cube and the cathedral.

The Stakes for the States

At the height of the recent European disaffection with the United States, I found myself in a long conversation over dinner with a close Polish friend and colleague. He was remembering the first, heady days of Solidarity, in which he'd been deeply engaged as a young student and activist. Why did it work, he wondered aloud? Where did Solidarity find the tensile strength to survive the martial law period and reemerge in the late 1980s as the only possible interlocutor for Poland's communist rulers? What was the glue that held together a national resistance coalition of workers and intellectuals, conservatives and liberals and radicals, peasants and bohemians, the pious and the skeptical?

The more he thought about it, the more it seemed to my friend that the answer could only be found in the realm of the spirit, in the domain of moral and spiritual truth. Reading history on the surface, you could explain Solidarity and the Revolution of 1989 in any number of conventional ways: the incapacities of communist economies, the clumsiness of communist governance, the rise of a generation of Polish and Soviet communist leaders who were willing to crack heads but were not going to roll in the tanks, the international protection afforded the Polish resistance by the fact of a Polish pope who had a global megaphone at his command, Western political and military pressure on the old USSR. But if you tried to explain it all *this* way, my friend argued, you simply didn't get the texture of the thing, the enormous excitement of those days, the dramatic sense of interior liberation, the exhilarating determination to live "as if" one were free, even if communism's institutional collapse was unimaginably far away.

The answer to the mystery of Solidarity and its entirely improbable victory had to lie elsewhere. The answer, to return to an image from Christopher Dawson, was beneath the surface of history. What made

Solidarity work, my friend finally concluded, was that millions of people, many of them non-Christian, committed themselves to living Christian values: the honesty that stood in sharp counterpoise to communism's lies about everything; the courage that faced up to communist brutality; the fraternity that resisted communism's attempts to divide and rule. Solidarity created a kind of new, or renewed, culture; that culture produced a new kind of resistance politics; the rest, as they say, is history.

My friend also suggested that this experience held lessons for Europe's twenty-first century, and for the question of Europe's relationship with the United States. If the twentieth century was, as John Paul II wrote in *Ecclesia in Europa,* a century of European loneliness and "inner emptiness," the Solidarity revolution was a moment when Europeans—first Poles, then others in east central Europe, then still others throughout the Continent—discovered that they weren't alone: that a "we" existed, a "we" that was capable of spiritual, moral, and political renewal. That European "we" lived an experience of solidarity in Solidarity, and the European "we" which lived that experience lived it in solidarity with American friends and allies. John Paul's epic pilgrimage to Poland in June 1979—nine days during which history turned in a different direction—provides a rough metaphor for the entire business: U.S.-funded Radio Free Europe broadcast John Paul's sermons and addresses on its Polish-language service 24/7, bringing the Polish pope to the Polish people over the heads of Poland's putative rulers, the whole thing being orchestrated by a Polish-American RFE leader who had been a hero of the Polish resistance during World War II.

Which may show something, I hope. Just as thoughtful Europeans and Americans today can recall a living experience of moral and political solidarity that transcended the hollow politics of expedience, utility, and *raison d'état*, significant numbers of Europeans have also had a living experience of cultural renewal leading to good political ends. Father Józef Tischner, the distinguished philosopher who served as chaplain of the first Solidarity Congress in Gdańsk in September 1981, used to describe Solidarity as "a huge forest planted by awakened consciences": a forest planted not in the classical age of the Roman martyrs nor in the Middle Ages but *today*.[86] If moral, spiritual, and cultural renewal was possible in Europe in the late twentieth century, isn't it possible to at least imagine a similar forest being planted across Europe in the twenty-first?

That possibility can be explored a bit more in a moment. Here, let me raise a question that some Americans ask, and in its bluntest form—so what? Or, to phrase it only a little less crudely, why should Americans care? Perhaps Europe will find within itself the resources for cultural and political renewal. Perhaps Europeans will even start having children again; good for them if they do. But if they don't, if Europe remains in civilizational crisis, what real effect does that have on the United States, beyond occasional aggravations at the U.N. Security Council? Let Europe continue to slide into a condition of powerlessness, eating its seed corn as it goes. What has any of that to do with us?

A lot, I believe. Because their "Europe problem" is also ours.

Why?

Aside from the enormous economic and other practical complications that an exhausted and imploding Europe will cause for the United States, and bracketing for the moment those aggravations at the Security Council, let me suggest three reasons why Americans should care. The first reason involves *pietas*, an ancient European, which is to say Roman, virtue, which teaches us both reverence and gratitude for those on whose shoulders we stand.

I'm prepared to argue that a lot of what has crossed the Atlantic in the past several centuries has been improved in the process: from the English language to forms of constitutional democracy to "rounders" (transformed by Americans into God's game, baseball). By the same token, *pietas* demands that I remember where all those good things came from in their original forms. A United States indifferent to the fate of Europe is a United States indifferent to its roots. Yes, Americans have developed a new form of European civilization. But that American civilization has long understood itself to be in continuity with the civilization of the West that we associate, in its origins, with Europe—with the unique civilizational accomplishment that emerged from the interaction of Jerusalem, Athens, and Rome.

Americans learned about the dignity of the human person, about limited and constitutional government, about the principle of consent, and about the transcendent standards of justice to which the state is accountable in the school of political culture—the school of freedom—that we call Europe. Americans should remember that, with *pietas*. We have seen what historical amnesia about cultural and civilizational roots has done to Europe, especially western Europe. Americans ought not to want that to happen in the United States.

The second reason we can and must care has to do with the medium- and long-term threat to American security posed by Europe's demographic meltdown.

Demographic vacuums do not remain unfilled—especially when the demographic vacuum in question is a continent possessed of immense economic resources. One can see the effects of Europe's self-inflicted depopulation in the tensions experienced in France, Germany, and elsewhere by rising tides of immigration from North Africa, Turkey, and other parts of the Islamic world. Since 1970, some 20 million (legal) Islamic immigrants—the equivalent of three E.U. countries, Ireland, Belgium, and Denmark—have settled in Europe.[87] And while, in the most optimistic of scenarios, these immigrants may become good European democrats, practicing civility and tolerance and committed to the religious freedom of all, there is another and far grimmer alternative, sketched in Fouad Ajami's portrait of the new "geography of Islam":

> The geography of Islam—and of the Islamic imagination—has shifted in recent years. The faith has become portable. Muslims who fled their countries brought Islam with them. Men came into *bilad al kufr* [the lands of unbelief], but a new breed of Islamists radicalized the faith there, in the midst of the *kafir* [unbeliever].
>
> The new lands were owed scant loyalty, if any, and political religious radicals savored the space afforded them by Western civil society. . . . You would

have thought that the pluralism and tumult of this open European world would spawn a version of the faith to match it. But precisely the opposite happened. In *bilad al kufr*, the faith became sharpened for battle. . . .

"A Muslim has no nationality except his belief," wrote an intellectual godfather of radical Islamism, the Egyptian Sayyid Qutb, who was executed by Nasser in 1966. While on a visit to Saudi Arabia in 2002, I listened to a caller from Stockholm [!] as he bared his concerns to an immensely popular preacher. He made Qutb's point: *We may carry their nationalities*, he said, *but we belong to our own religion.* . . . [88]

Thus Europe's current demographic trend lines, coupled with the radicalization of Islam that seems to be a by-product of some Muslims' encounter with contemporary, secularized Europe, could eventually produce a Europe in which Polish King Jan III Sobieski's victory at Vienna in 1683 is reversed, such that the Europe of the twenty-second century, or even the late twenty-first, is a Europe increasingly influenced, and perhaps even dominated, by militant Islamic populations, convinced that their long-delayed triumph in the European heartland is at hand.

We have already seen what the emergence of significant Islamic populations has done to the politics of France. Is there no connection between the problems posed domestically in France by its new immigrant population, on the one hand, and the strategy of appeasement toward radicalized Islam in the world adopted by French political leaders, on the other? It seems very unlikely. Within a few decades, the majority of teenagers in the Netherlands will be Muslims; what will happen to the politics of the Netherlands when those teenagers become voting adults? Is a European future dominated by an appeasement mentality toward radical Islamism in the best interests of the United States? That too seems unlikely. Neither is a Europe that is a breeding ground for Islamic radicalism; remember that the experience of life in Hamburg was decisive in the evolution of both Mohammed Atta, leader of the 9/11 death pilots, and of the pilot of the fourth plane of that grim day, the plane forced down in Shanksville, Pennsylvania—the plane intended to hit the Capitol or the White House.

The third reason why the "Europe problem" is ours as well as theirs has to do with the future of the democratic project in the United States and indeed throughout the world. What Pierre Manent laments as

Europe's "depoliticization" already has its parallels in American public life. What was most disturbing, for example, about the bizarre debate over the mere mention of Christianity's contributions to European civilization in the proposed European constitution was that the amnesiacs who wanted to rewrite European history by eliminating Christianity from the historical equation were doing so in service to a thin, indeed anorexic, idea of procedural democracy. To deny that Christianity had anything to do with the evolution of free, law-governed, and prosperous European societies is, as I've argued above, more than a question of falsifying the past; it is also a matter of creating a future in which moral truth has no role in governance, in the determination of public policy, in understandings of justice, and in the definition of that freedom which democracy is intended to embody.

Were these ideas to triumph in Europe, that would be bad news for Europe; but it would also be bad news for the United States, for that triumph would inevitably reinforce similar tendencies in our own high culture, and ultimately in our law. The judicial redefinition of freedom as personal willfulness manifest in the 2003 Supreme Court decision *Lawrence v. Texas* was buttressed by citations from European courts. And what would it mean for the democratic project in global terms if the notion that democracy has nothing to do with moral truth is exported from western Europe to central and eastern Europe via the expanded European Union, and thence to other new democracies around the world? If Christopher Dawson was right that a thoroughly secularized democracy, constitutionally and politically disabled from bringing transcendent moral truths to bear on its public life, is self-destructive, then the entire democratic project—in Latin America, in south and east Asia, in Oceania and Canada—is being imperiled by the prospect that the "Europe problem" will metastasize beyond the European Union's current membership.

So there are many reasons why Americans should, and must, care. We sever ourselves from our civilizational roots if we ignore Europe in a fit of aggravation or pique. Our security will be further imperiled in a post–9/11 world if Europe's demographics continue to change in ways that give new advantage to the dynamism of radical Islamism in world politics. The American democratic experiment will be weakened if Europe's depoliticization reinforces similar tendencies in the United States, and so will the democratic project in the world.

Futures

Back, then, to Europe. What are Europe's possible futures? How will the newly expanded European Union evolve in the first decades of the twenty-first century? Prognostications of this sort are notoriously dicey. But a reading of current European history from beneath the surface of that history suggests four plausible scenarios.

Paradise Works

The first possibility is that the Europe embodied in current E.U. practice and envisioned in the new European constitution actually works: Europe continues to prosper economically, successfully integrates its new

member states and its expanding immigrant populations, expands even farther into the former Yugoslavia
and perhaps into several former Soviet republics, solves
the problem of Turkey's controversial request for ad-
mission, demonstrates the possibilities of "soft power"
in world politics, and is free from destructive, destabi-
lizing terrorist attacks. That would seem to be the European future imagined by Romano Prodi, Valéry
Giscard d'Estaing, and other vocal proponents of the
new Europe and its difference, especially when compared with the United States.

And it could, perhaps, happen. But realistic Europeans and, one suspects, most of the Americans who
pay any serious attention to these questions regard it as
a very long shot indeed.

Europe's future economic prosperity requires a rediscovery of the work ethic, liberation from the con-
straints of national and transnational bureaucracies,
the rebirth of entrepreneurship, and a dramatic solution to the problem of unfunded pension liabilities and
other health care and social welfare programs—and
none of these seems likely at the moment.

Successful integration of the ten new E.U. member
states may go smoothly, although the political and indeed psychological tensions just below the surface of
equanimity and *fraternité* were evident in the run-up to

the 2003 Iraq War, when French President Jacques
Chirac read the riot act to several pro-American new
democracies in east central Europe, telling them in no
uncertain terms to mind their manners and defer to
their elders and betters. Still, the integration of its new
member states seems less daunting a task for Europe
than the successful assimilation of its immigrants—especially those Islamic immigrants who, as Fouad Ajami
has noted, become radicalized by living among the infidels, not to mention already-radicalized Islamists who
come to Europe and see in today's migration patterns
the beginning of the rightful reclamation of Europe for
the true faith. How will a Europe constitutionally committed to "neutrality toward worldviews" find within itself the moral resources to live in tolerance and civility
as the social and political pressures that will inevitably
accompany an expanding Islamic population inside
western Europe intensify? What will a Europe committed to secularity in its public life do with people whose
presence in Europe is economically essential but whose
outlook is resolutely, even aggressively, unsecular?

Indeed, while the benign future envisioned by Romano Prodi, Valéry Giscard d'Estaing and others seems
to assume that Muslims will become secularized and
utilitarian in their approach to public life, the likelier

probability is that this benign future will depend on Europe (and the rest of the democratic world, including the United States) facilitating a kind of development of social doctrine in Islam, in which Muslims themselves develop an Islamic case for tolerance, civility, and pluralism. This will not, to put it gently, be an easy business. Islam abhors the Christian notion of the trinitarian God, judging the Christian doctrine of the Trinity to be polytheism; yet a case can be made that this "pluralistic" understanding of the Godhead was a crucial factor in Christian societies' affirmation of social pluralism. Similarly, the Christian doctrine of Creation, which stresses God's ongoing creative action in history, helped set the cultural stage for the emergence of a politics of persuasion in Christian-influenced societies. Islam, by contrast, is radically voluntaristic and will-centered, a theological optic on reality that tends to underwrite a politics of coercion. That no Islamic society save Turkey, which (forcefully) took Islam out of public life, has developed into a pluralistic democracy is not simply an accident of history; it reflects the deep theological and doctrinal structure of Islam. Thus the development of an Islamic "social doctrine" capable of sustaining tolerance, civility, and pluralism engages the most serious questions of Islamic self-understanding and reminds us that great social and political questions are, more often than not, ultimately theological in character.

The question of Turkey and the European Union is a thorny one that may exacerbate tensions with the United States, which, to date, has taken the position that a faithful NATO ally like Turkey belongs in Europe. On the one hand, Turkey is a secular democracy; and the argument could, and doubtless will, be made that Turkey's accession to the European Union could have a positive influence on the problem of assimilating large numbers of Islamic immigrants into western European societies. On the other hand, western Europe's demographic demise, coupled with Turkey's expanding population, holds out the prospect of a Europe in the mid–twenty first century in which Turkey has the largest say in E.U. affairs, given E.U. constitutional arrangements. Then there is the further question of whether the European Union wants its eastern border to abut Syria and Iraq.

As for terrorism and its impact on the evolving European Union, it seems unlikely that appeasement strategies will work indefinitely. Perhaps Europeans are right in suggesting that 9/11 and the Madrid bombings were the result of inept American policy in the Middle East, and that a Europe increasingly distancing itself from the United States will be able to maintain its distance from Islamist wrath. On the other hand, if 9/11, Madrid, and the bombings in Istanbul in 2003 represent, from the Islamist point of view, moments in a larger struggle against the West and its culture—a struggle that has gone on for centuries and in which there are Islamic defeats to be avenged (as in Spain in 1492, Lepanto in 1571, and Vienna in 1683)—it is not easy to see how Europe can, in effect, drop out of twenty-first century history and pursue Robert Kagan's Kantian paradise of perpetual peace on its own.

Finally, there is the question of whether a Europe continuing down its present path has the cultural resources necessary to make the Europe envisioned in the draft European constitution work. In the aftermath of the June 2004 meeting in which it was agreed, once again, to omit any reference to the Christian roots of European civilization from the Euro-constitution's preamble, Pope John Paul II said, with some asperity, "One does not cut off the roots from which one is born."[89] Trees cut off from their roots die. Do political projects and civilizations do the same?

There are no guarantees in history, so perhaps one ought to hold out the theoretical possibility that Europe can be made to work as the drafters of the Euro-constitution imagine—as a secular political space built on neutrality toward worldviews and a resolute resistance to religiously informed moral argument within the European public square. But isn't the task made even more difficult by the fact that this neutrality is not, as we have seen, really neutrality at all, but rather a deep-set hostility to one of the thickest roots from which Europe has grown? Is there any other instance in history of a successful political project built on such a deliberate rupture with the project's historic cultural foundations?

The Muddle

The second possibility is that Europe muddles through, with different European countries adopting different solutions to what may well be Europe's most urgent problem: the population meltdown in western Europe and the filling of the consequent demographic vacuum by Islamic immigration. British historian Niall Ferguson correctly notes that "most European Muslims are, of course, law-abiding citizens with little sympathy for terrorist attacks on European cities." Still, he continues, there is no question that Europe is "experiencing fundamental demographic and cultural changes whose long-term consequences no one can foresee. . . . A youthful Muslim society to the south and east of the

Mediterranean is poised to colonize—the term is not too strong—a senescent Europe."[90]

Despite Europe's increasing economic and political integration, the European response to this "colonization" could well vary from country to country. To cite Niall Ferguson again:

> A creeping Islamicization of a decadent Christendom is one conceivable result: while the old Europeans get even older and their religious faith weaker, the Muslim colonies within their cities get larger and more overt in their religious observance. A backlash against immigration by the economically Neanderthal right is another: aging electorates turn to demagogues who offer sealed borders without explaining exactly who is to pay for the pensions and health care. Nor can we rule out the possibility of a happy fusion between rapidly secularized second-generation Muslims and their post-Christian neighbors. Indeed, we may conceivably end up with all three: Situation 1 in France, Situation 2 in Austria, and Situation 3 in Britain.[91]

So it could be a muddle. But suppose significant parts of Europe were to violate E.U. commitments to continental openness—for example, by challenging the E.U. commitment to a Continent-wide job market with a free flow of peoples across traditional national borders? This would not be the Europe imagined by today's enthusiastic European integrators. And any chance of a coordinated pan-European approach to world politics in general and the Islamist/terrorist threat in particular will be very difficult to achieve if Europe takes a variety of tacks in dealing with its demographic future.

Europe Reconverted

The drama of atheistic humanism does not exhaust the story of Christianity and nineteenth-century Europe; nor is the story of exclusive humanism and its grip on contemporary European high culture all there is to twentieth- and twenty-first-century Europe. While Christianity in nineteenth-century Europe was wrestling with the intellectual challenge of atheistic humanism, it was also sending thousands of missionaries to Africa, Latin America, and Asia. If, as some have suggested, the old metropolitan centers of Europe are reevangelized from their former African colonies in the twenty-first century, it will be because of the tremendous evangelical energies Europe poured into Africa in the nineteenth century. As the drama of atheistic humanism was taking its most lethal form in Europe in the mid–twentieth century, great Christian witnesses like

Karl Barth, Dietrich Bonhoeffer, and Edith Stein were being raised up—in the latter two cases, to become martyrs, as were hundreds of thousands of European Christians under Nazism and communism. As a softer, but scarcely less assertive, exclusive humanism sought to prevent Christianity from resuming any significant role in the formation of European public culture in Cold War Europe, new movements of Christian renewal sprang to life, from the world-renowned ecumenical community at Taizé in France to such Catholic movements as Focolare (which quietly helped keep Christianity alive behind the Iron Curtain) and Opus Dei (which played an important role in Spain's transition from dictatorship to democracy). As most Europeans turned away from the active practice of Christian faith, still millions of others kept alive the ancient European tradition of pilgrimage—to Fatima, Lourdes, Częstochowa, Mariazell, Assisi, or San Giovanni Rotondo, home of the Franciscan stigmatic, Padre Pio. As we have seen, self-consciously Christian statesmen laid the foundations of today's European Union, and Christian conviction played a crucial role in the Revolution of 1989, the end of the Cold War, and the re-creation of the possibility of a Europe in full.

So the picture is not monochromatic, nor is the story line necessarily that of a one-way street leading to a dead end. Modern European history can be read from one angle as a history of apostasy—a deliberate, self-conscious detachment of the present and future from Europe's Christian roots. But modern European history can also be read from another angle, as a history of missionaries, saints, statesmen, men and women of genius, and martyrs—a history of great spiritual dynamism amid rapidly advancing secularization.

So a third possible European future can be imagined: Europe is reconverted and finds in Christianity—especially the social doctrine of the Catholic Church—the spiritual, intellectual, and moral resources to sustain and defend its commitments to toleration, civility, democracy, and human rights.

This scenario seems to have guided thinking in the Vatican for years: an integrating Europe will be forced to ask the question of the sources of its unity, which can only be answered, ultimately, by Christianity. Thus the most enthusiastic Europeans in the Vatican have seen, in the European Union and its expansion, an evangelical opportunity—an opportunity to reverse the centuries-long process of European secularization: Brussels, setting out to make the rest of Europe Belgium, in fact succeeds in making the rest of Europe Poland.

Sociologist Andrew Greeley warns against using secularization as an all-purpose brush with which to paint a portrait of contemporary Europe, arguing from survey research that Europe is not monolithic and that many, perhaps most, Europeans still affirm beliefs in God or some divine force in the world. Yet as historian Philip Jenkins noted in a review of Greeley's work, "Greeley's surveys show Europeans agreeing in large numbers with certain beliefs and assertions, but with little sense of the strength or cultural meaning of those statements."[92] No one who has spent a Sunday morning in Munich (or London, Paris, Madrid, Milan, or Lisbon, not to mention Amsterdam, Copenhagen, or Stockholm) in the past twenty years will imagine that Christian conviction plays a significant role in the way many, perhaps most, western Europeans conduct their lives, whatever they may tell pollsters about their private religious musings.

Sunday morning in Kraków is different, however; as a friend noted in July 2004, when we were together in that beautiful place, "It's remarkable to be in a city in which the principal activity on Sunday morning is going to Mass." And here is one possibility for the reconversion of Europe, its rediscovery of its spiritual roots, and the consequent strengthening of its democratic political culture: the religiously more intense societies of east central Europe, with living memories of religiously shaped democratic political change, may, as new members of the European Union, reignite a "new evangelization" (as Pope John Paul II has termed it) in the older democracies of post-Christian western Europe.

This, to be sure, is not a certain thing. No one knows what will happen, for example, in Poland—arguably the world's most intensely Catholic country—when billions of euros flood into the country in various E.U.–sponsored economic development projects and cultural initiatives. No one knows what will happen in Poland now that John Paul II has left the scene, after decades of reminding his countrymen of who they are and from whence they came. On the other hand, the vitality of Polish Catholicism—a vitality mirrored, if not quite so exuberantly, in some other central and eastern European countries—could reenergize the often somnambulant local churches of western Europe. Increasing contacts across the old Iron Curtain could help make it clear to western European Church leaders, intellectuals, and activists that modernization doesn't necessarily mean the wholesale marginalization of Christian conviction from personal, familial, and public life (which is a definition of "secularization" on which everyone could perhaps agree).

There is also a generational issue in play in western Europe. I've mentioned the generation of 1968 and its impact on western European culture and politics—and now on the definition of Europe. Much to this generation's surprise, and chagrin, its children are not following uniformly in its footsteps. As I said above, I first became aware of this in 1997 in Paris. To the amazement of most of French high culture, the international Catholic World Youth Day, held in Paris in August 1997, was an overwhelming success: 500,000 young adults participated in a week of talks, conversations, and religious services, and more than a million people packed themselves into the Longchamp race course for a closing papal Mass. Throughout the week, John Paul II and other Catholic leaders had driven home the message: sanctity is possible in modernity; Catholic faith can nurture a free society *(liberté)*, human dignity *(egalité)*, and human solidarity *(fraternité)*. The response was overwhelming.

And confusing, at least to some. The night of the closing Mass, Cardinal Jean-Marie Lustiger of Paris, who had long argued that Europe must be reconverted "from the head down" (i.e., through a new evangelization of intellectuals and youth), appeared on French national television. The anchorman, a child of 1968 straight out of central casting, asked the cardinal to explain the inexplicable: why, in the middle of summer holidays, had this vast crowd come to Paris to *pray*? Lustiger was blunt. It was a question of generations, he insisted. The anchorman belonged to a generation that had abandoned the Church of its youth in 1968 or thereabouts and had been fighting daddy, as it were, ever since. These young people, the cardinal continued, grew up empty. Having found Christ and the Church, they wanted to explore everything that meant. Don't read their experience, Lustiger told his startled inter-locutor, through yours: these young men and women don't think that being Christian and being intelligent, engaged, compassionate, and dedicated are mutually exclusive.

No one would argue that World Youth Day 1997—and its equivalents in Spain (1989), Poland (1991), and Rome (2000)—have decisively reshaped the cultural landscape of Europe. Yet the millions of young people who have participated in these events now form a po-tentially powerful European network of friendship and collaboration across old national and ethnic borders and antipathies. In the next two decades, they will come into their own politically—if they have the will and nerve for leadership. Many of them are associated with Catholic renewal movements that form another associational grid across Europe: movements like Communion and Liberation, the Sant'Egidio Community, the Emmanuel Community, Regnum Christi, and the two previously mentioned, Focolare and Opus Dei.[93] Many Catholic leaders believe that the future of the Church in western Europe rests with these renewal movements: if Europe rediscovers its Christian roots, senior bishops suggest, it will be through these movements rather than through the often sclerotic structures of institutional Catholicism.

Again, no one knows whether this will happen. And even if the seeds John Paul II planted in young souls in the late twentieth and early twenty-first centuries were to blossom in decades to come, the question remains of how much more damage the 1968 generation will do to Europe's self-understanding before the children of the children of 1968 achieve anything like cultural critical mass. Still, it would be unwise to imagine European futures without imagining the possibility that the "John Paul II generation" just might reconnect Europe to the deepest-running source of its unique civilization.

Were that to happen, the public consequences would be substantial—not in recreating state churches but in offering an alternative to contemporary Europe's soul-withering fascination with the state as church.[94]

1683 Reversed

Then there is the nightmare scenario—nightmarish, at least, for those who cherish the unique contributions of European civilization to world civilization and affirm the noble aspirations in the preamble to the European constitution.

In this scenario, western Europe fails to reverse its demographic decline; its finances become ever more perilous, its native populations ever more demoralized, and its more recent arrivals ever more assertively Islamic. The "new evangelization" has not taken hold; the democracies of east central Europe have failed to ignite a renewal of European interest in the adventure of democracy, having themselves become less intensely religious as they become further enmeshed in the cords of the Euro-bureaucracy. As Europe becomes, in Niall Ferguson's term, more "senescent," the European Union becomes more sclerotic, unable to grapple with great decisions. A tipping point is finally reached—through a combination of demographic, financial, social, cultural, and political factors—and the grand project of Europe collapses. Some states of east central Europe retain their Christian culture and their democracy. Most of western Europe becomes Islamicized, not in the senses suggested above under the "muddle through" scenario, but in the sense of being drawn into the civilizational orbit of the Arab Islamic world—which has, from its point of view, finally reversed the defeat of the Ottomans in 1683 at the gates of Vienna. Non-Muslim western Europeans become *dhimmis*, second-class citizens with no effective role in public life.

Some will say that this simply cannot happen. In fact, though, something like it has happened before. By the seventh century, the once flourishing Greco-Roman-Christian civilization of North Africa had been severely weakened by theological and ecclesiastical controversies that sapped its civilizational strength and attenuated its ability to "give an account"—to persuade itself that its civilizational accomplishment could and should be defended. Within eight brief decades, that civilization disappeared into the sands. It was militarily destroyed by the advancing armies of Islam, and the political/military incapacities of both the western and eastern wings of Christianity certainly played a role in North African Christianity's virtual extinction. Yet one cannot help thinking that the foundations had been eroded before the armies of the Prophet appeared.

Were something similar to happen in Europe in the late twenty-first or early twenty-second century, it might not be—indeed it likely would not be—because an Islamist army marched into western Europe and conquered it. It wouldn't have to. Europe—in the sense of the civilizational enterprise we identify with the interaction of Jerusalem, Athens, and Rome, a civilization whose modern democratic public life was prepared in the Christian high culture of the Middle Ages—would have handed itself over to its new populations. In significant parts of Europe, the drama of atheistic humanism would have played itself out in the triumph of a thoroughly nonhumanistic theism. The crisis of civilizational morale that Europe is experiencing today would have reached its bitter end in a Europe in which the muezzin summons the faithful to prayer from the central loggia of St. Peter's in Rome, while Notre-Dame has been transformed into Hagia Sophia on the Seine—a great Christian church become an Islamic museum.

If the cathedral goes this way, the human rights celebrated by the cube will be in the gravest jeopardy. The democratic lights would indeed go out over much of Europe, and the kind of darkness that followed would be beyond Sir Edward Grey's imagining.

Reversing the Question

As I bring this meditation on Europe and America to a close, let me stress once again that the concerns expressed here about Europe's future are not caused by some crude American Europhobia, nor are they the product of the sharp division between much of Europe and the United States over the Iraq War. Iraq may have brought to a head, for many Americans, the questions of what Europe has become, and what the future of the transatlantic relationship will be. My purpose here has been to probe beneath those questions and ask why Europe seems to be in a crisis of civilizational morale, the most disturbing manifestations of which are not to be found in French or

German policy toward Iraq but in the unprecedented phenomenon of European depopulation, coupled with what acute European observers like Pierre Manent describe as Europe's flight from politics.

This crisis of civilizational morale was also evident in the rather bland response many Europeans made to the enlargement of the European Union in May 2004. Enlargement on this scale—which involved bringing a number of former Warsaw Pact countries into Europe, thus further underscoring the reunification of the Continent in the aftermath of the Cold War—ought to have been an occasion of great satisfaction and celebration. Not only were the horrors of the twentieth century being overcome; so were nationalist divisions that had riven Europe for centuries. But there seemed to be considerable public anxiety about Europe rather than a widespread sense of satisfaction, and what celebrations there were looked rather muted.

Which may suggest that, among Europeans themselves, the deeper question of their future—reconciliation and unification *for what?*—is starting to be raised. Europe has successfully traversed the difficult path from the Coal and Steel Community to the Common Market to the enlarged European Union. But is that all there is? Perhaps, inside Europe itself, there is an intuition that a Europe of political, legal, and economic structures alone is insufficient, or at least not as satisfying an achievement as might have been expected. Europe's horizon of expectation about itself seems to have become drastically foreshortened, and thoughtful Europeans are asking whether a Europe that represents, in the main, the Continent-wide triumph of bureaucratic regulation is all that can be hoped for.

The debate over whether the new European constitution should acknowledge the Christian sources of European political culture was important in its own right: it clarified—if in a disturbing way—how important figures in the high culture of Europe, as well as many influential European political leaders, think about their past. The debate was also about the present and the future, however. Those who insisted most vehemently that there be no overt recognition that Christianity played a decisive role in the formation of European civilization did not do so in the name of tolerance, claims to the contrary notwithstanding. They did so because they are committed to the proposition that there can be politics without God: that a Europe free, tolerant, civil, and pluralistic can only be built as a public space from which the God of the Bible has been excluded.*

---

*Judging from the Buttiglione case, which roiled European political and journalistic circles in late 2004, it seems that orthodox

(continues)

That this position is shared by more than a few American political, judicial, intellectual, and cultural leaders is obvious, and suggests that what has been unfolding in Europe in recent decades—indeed, over the past two centuries—could well be replicated in the United States (and already is being replicated in Canada). To repeat, that is why "their" Europe problem is, from an American point of view, "our" problem too.

All of which involves a great reversal. From 1789 on, the question of Christianity and democracy was usually posed like this: Could the various Christian confessions accommodate themselves to pluralistic democracy? In the course of that "accommodation," more than a few Christian communities lost the capac-

---

(continued)

Christians are also to be excluded from the new Europe's public space, or at least its public offices.

Rocco Buttiglione, a distinguished Italian philosopher and Minister for European Affairs in the Italian government, was chosen by the incoming president of the European Commission, Portugal's Jose Manuel Durao Barroso, to be commissioner of justice on the new Commission. Professor Buttiglione was then subjected to a particularly nasty inquisition by the justice committee of the European Parliament. His convictions about the morality of homosexual acts and the nature of marriage were deemed by Euro-parliamentarians to disqualify him from holding high office on the European Commission—despite Buttiglione's clear distinction, in his testimony, between what

ity to play a significant role as moral counselors in public life. Yet others became crucial actors in the defeat of communist totalitarianism and the creation of free societies in east central Europe. And on a worldwide basis, the Catholic Church, long thought incapable of accepting democracy as anything other than a tolerable way station en route to the restoration of confessional states, has become arguably the world's foremost institutional promoter of the democratic project. It was not, after all, a European political leader who twice, in the last quarter of the twentieth century, stood at the rostrum of the U.N. General Assembly and made a passionate defense of the universality of human rights; it was the 264th Bishop of Rome, the Supreme Pontiff of the Catholic Church. Whatever else remains

---

he, a committed and intellectually sophisticated Catholic, regards as immoral behavior and what the law regards as criminal behavior, and despite his sworn commitment, substantiated by a lifetime of work, to uphold and defend the legitimate civil rights of all. This did not satisfy many members of the European parliament, who evidently agreed with one of their number in his claim that Buttiglione's moral convictions—not any actions he had undertaken, and would likely undertake, but his *convictions*—were "in direct contradiction of European law."

Buttiglione described this to a British newspaper as the "new totalitarianism," which is not, I fear, an exaggeration. That this new totalitarianism flies under the flag of "tolerance" only makes matters worse.

unsettled, the old question of Christianity and democracy would seem to have been answered.

Only to be followed, however, by a new question that reverses the polarities. The question lurking beneath the European constitutional debate stood the old question on its head. Now, it seems, the question before the house is this: Is it possible to construct and sustain a democratic political community absent the transcendent moral reference points for ordering public life that Christianity offers the political community? Can there be a "politics" fit for human beings without God—the God of Abraham, Isaac, Jacob, and Jesus?

Those who won that particular debate in Europe in 2004 would answer in the affirmative: yes, not only can there be politics without God, there must be politics without God. The European crisis of civilizational morale suggests, however, that the winners of the European constitutional debate are seriously mistaken.

The Cost of Boredom

In an article on early–twenty-first-century Christianity in Europe and America, published just when the Euro-constitution debate was entering its final phase, Orthodox theologian David Hart wrote that it seemed to him "fairly obvious that there is some direct, indissoluble bond between faith and the will to a future, or between the desire for a future and the imagination of eternity." No faith, no future: "This is why post-Christian Europe seems to lack not only the moral and imaginative resources for sustaining its civilization, but even any good reason for continuing to reproduce." As for the enlarged European Union, Hart found it difficult to think that it was likely to generate "some great cultural renewal that might inspire a new zeal for having children."[95]

Both American and European friends and colleagues with whom I have discussed these questions understandably find it hard to accept what they regard as a too simple, even simplistic notion: that Europe has stopped reproducing itself because most Europeans have stopped going to church. And put that baldly, the analysis is too simple. Of course there are economic, sociological, psychological, and even ideological reasons why Europe's birthrates have fallen below replacement level for decades. But the failure to create a human future in the most elemental sense—by creating a successor generation—is surely an expression of a broader failure: a failure of self-confidence. That broader failure is no less surely tied to a collapse of faith in the God of the Bible. For when God goes—and the death of the biblical God in the European public square is what today's European actors in the ongoing drama of atheistic humanism seek and have to a significant measure accomplished—so does God's first command: "Be fruitful and multiply" (Genesis 1:28).

In place of Europe's quondam faith in the God of the Bible, which withered under the fierce assault of atheistic humanism, the kinder, gentler exclusive humanism of contemporary European high culture has enshrined various secularist deities: tolerance, which it misunderstands as indifference; pluralism, which it imagines to be a mere sociological fact rather than a cultural achievement; *laïcité*, and all the rest. But the worship of these substitute gods has drastically lowered Europe's moral and historical horizon. In domestic affairs, as Pierre Manent and others have warned, the Continent has wandered into a postpolitical wilderness in which the authority to settle virtually all the hard issues has been delegated to transnational courts and the Brussels bureaucracy. Hand in hand with this arrangement of public life—itself the by-product of statism and a softer form of socialism—goes a (sometimes cheerfully) nihilistic attitude toward the idea of any transcendent standard of judgment (or justice) by which public life is to be ordered.

In international affairs, the situation seems much the same. Over and above the specific disagreements Europeans have with U.S. policy in the global war against terrorism, and far beyond the disagreements between Europe and the United States over Iraq, one senses in many European cultural and political leaders an instinctive recoil from, even a horror at, the idea that freedom is a gift from God that must be actively defended—as George W. Bush frequently dared to put it, thus earning himself even more opprobrium from

Europe's *bien-pensants* (and at least one cardinal of the Catholic Church, Germany's Karl Lehmann). Unapologetic confessions of religious faith by Americans, and especially by American political leaders, are dismissed by many Europeans today as evidence of fanaticism, xenophobia, and aggression—and thus, in a perverse example of displacement, are made to substitute for the danger that dare not be named: the Islamist threat now inside Europe's house.

How to account for all this? David Hart suggests that the problem is boredom—not simply boredom of the day-in, day-out, quotidian sort but boredom on a transcendent, even metaphysical plane: a kind of boredom with the mystery of life itself. His indictment is unsparing:

> A culture—a civilization—is only as great as the religious ideas that animate it; the magnitude of a people's cultural achievement is determined by the height of its spiritual aspirations. One need only turn one's gaze to the frozen mires and fetid marshes of modern Europe, where once the greatest of human civilizations resided, to grasp how devastating and omnivorous a power metaphysical boredom is. The eye of faith presumes to see something miraculous within the ordinariness of the moment, mysterious hints of

an intelligible order calling out for translation into artifacts, but boredom's disenchantment renders the imagination inert and desire torpid.[96]

Is the answer to Europe's metaphysical boredom—and its corrosive effects on Europe's emerging continental public life—a return to something like the Middle Ages? No. That is impossible and would be undesirable if it were possible. The answer may lie, however, in a different way of reading the modern project. European secularists insist that a modern understanding of the human condition implies a radical skepticism that often expresses itself as atheism—once a sort of heroic (if often perversely heroic) atheism; now, in David Hart's pungent phrase, "metaphysical boredom." But suppose there is another way—a "more excellent way"?

A Different Modernity

Sometime in 2004, a European poll—or perhaps it was a contest—revealed that a significant number of Europeans thought that Karol Wojtyła, Pope John Paul II, was the emblematic "European" of our times. However satisfying that might have been to the late pope's friends, it also seemed, on reflection, a little odd. For it is no secret that the most difficult reception of John Paul II's teaching, indeed the most difficult reception of his entire pontificate, was in Europe. Why?

The conventional explanation is that John Paul II and the Catholicism he proclaimed reflected a premodern cast of mind that ill fits the contemporary world. But this does not square with the evidence. John Paul II was, in fact, the first modern pope, the first pope whose intellectual architecture was modern, not classical. Pope Paul VI (1963–1978) is sometimes called the "first modern pope," but when he reached for a literary allusion, it was usually to Augustine. When John Paul II reached for a literary allusion, it was often to Paul Ricoeur, Emmanuel Levinas, or other thoroughly modern European philosophers. John Paul II did not propose a return to the premodern world. Rather, he offered a thoroughly modern alternative reading of modernity. John Paul II's thought and his teaching were a challenge to look at the modern world, its triumphs and its struggles, through a different and perhaps more acute lens; they are a challenge to cleanse ourselves of metaphysical boredom and rediscover the mystery and adventure of being. It is a challenge that Europeans and Americans alike ought to take seriously, for accepting that challenge and engaging this "different modernity," this Christian account of modernity, may be crucial, even essential, to the democratic project and the defense of freedom.

How to begin engaging that challenge? As good a way as any is to have a look at *Fidei Depositum* (1992), the "apostolic constitution" (the highest form of papal teaching authority) with which John Paul II issued the *Catechism of the Catholic Church*. In that very personal document, John Paul wrote of the "symphony of truth." As a European who was first and foremost a disciple of Jesus Christ, and as a scholar who analyzed classic Christian doctrine with contemporary intellectual tools and methods, Karol Wojtyła was convinced that Christian faith is a unity. The Creed is neither a random inventory of truth claims nor a "system" constructed by human ingenuity. Rather, Christian faith for John Paul II was a unified understanding of the human condition that begins in God's revelation, which is the source of doctrine and the starting point of theology. Here John Paul reflected an ancient Catholic sensibility. In the "symphony of truth" that is Christian faith, the "instruments" that make up the ensemble do not perform in a haphazard or incoherent way, but support each other in a melodic structure that, by its very nature, demands to be engaged as a whole.

This "symphony of truth" includes moral truth.

From his first steps as a professorial lecturer in moral philosophy in the 1950s through the early years of the twenty-first century, Karol Wojtyła challenged skeptics and relativists who may grudgingly concede that, in matters of the moral life (which includes public life), there may be "your" truth and "my" truth but there is certainly no such thing as *the* truth. John Paul II had an alternative view of our moral circumstances.

He was convinced that a careful philosophical reflection on human moral agency—how we make our moral judgments and act on them—discloses truths that are built into the world and into human beings: truths that are necessary food for the human mind and soul, truths we ignore at grave peril to ourselves and to the human project.

In this judgment, as in many others, John Paul II challenged the metaphysically bored and their conviction that things just can't be put together in a coherent way. On the contrary, John Paul urged, modern men and women are not condemned to live in a world that is fragmented, cut off from the past, and ultimately incomprehensible. There is an alternative reading of modernity, a different way to be modern. And that, John Paul II was convinced, is what the Second Vatican Council intended the Catholic Church to propose: a rereading of the contemporary situation in which the modern world's intense reflection on the human person is revitalized through an encounter with Jesus Christ, who reveals both the face of the merciful Father *and* the true meaning of our humanity. Christian humanism is a thoroughly modern alternative to both atheistic humanism and exclusive humanism—a thoroughly modern understanding of the human condition that has not willfully cut itself off from western civilization's roots.

The high adventure of Christian orthodoxy is one alternative to metaphysical boredom.

Like other prescient European Catholic intellectuals, John Paul II understood that secularization—which certainly entails metaphysical boredom—is not a neutral phenomenon. A thoroughly secularized world is a world without windows, doors, or skylights: a claustrophobic, ultimately suffocating world. A thoroughly secularized culture from which transcendent reference points for human thought and action have disappeared is bad for the cause of human freedom and democracy because democracy, in the final analysis, rests on the conviction that the human person possesses an inalienable dignity and value and that freedom is not mere willfulness. Even before one gets to these public or systemic issues, however, a thoroughly secularized world is bad for human beings. "Silence," a prominent German bishop and theologian once put it to me, "is stifling: human beings cannot live with the silence"—the silence of a world without the "still, small voice" that spoke to Elijah in history, from beyond history (see 1 Kings 19:12).

This brings us back to John Paul II's alternative reading of the modern condition and his Christian humanism. In the late pope's vision of the human person and of history, the question of God is central precisely because the question of man is central. To ask the question of man is, inevitably, to raise the question of God. To try to read the course of history without God is to read history in a shallow way, because God's search for man and the human response to that divine quest is the central reality of history. To ask the great humanistic question—What is man, and how does the human person function in history?—is to confront the question of God. A true anthropology, a true human-ism, speaks of God and man, and thus liberates men and women from the stifling confines of "the silence."

These convictions about Christ-centered humanism are the key to understanding John Paul II's effect on the history of our times—and to grasping the possibil-ity of a "different modernity" capable of resolving Eu-rope's crisis of civilizational morale. It was precisely because of his convictions about God, Christ, culture, and history that John Paul II could ignite the revolution of conscience in central and eastern Europe that we now know as the Revolution of 1989. It was precisely because John Paul was convinced that God is central to the human story that he could, by calling men and women to religious and moral conversion, give them tools of resistance that communism could not blunt. It was precisely because John Paul II understood that Christianity is not a form of religious Idealism existing somewhere outside history that he could call people to solidarity *in* history—and thus change the course of history. Stalin's famously derisive challenge to the papacy, "How many divisions has the pope?" was met by a man who knew and understood the power of truth in history, which is another way of describing the power of God in history. Surely this recent lesson, which is within the living memory of adult Europeans and Americans, is worth conjuring with as Europe ponders its meaning and its future—and as Americans try to understand what Europe's current malaise may portend about their own future.

The Cube and the Cathedral

So we come, once again, to the question of the cube and the cathedral. Which culture is more likely to protect human rights, promote the common good, defend legitimate pluralism, and give an account of the moral commitments that make democracy possible—the culture that produced the coldly rationalistic Grande Arche de la Défense? Or the culture embodied in the cathedral that the proponents of La Grande Arche imagine fitting neatly within their cube? La Grande Arche embodies, if in a visually striking way, metaphysical boredom; it speaks to us of politics without God, indeed it celebrates politics without God as a great liberation for humanity. The holy unsameness of

Notre-Dame, with its combination of stately stone and luminous glass, embodies, by contrast, the openness of the human spirit to the transcendent—to God. It took a long time for the people who built the cathedral to articulate, from within their own religious convictions, a persuasive, compelling case for democracy. But they have done that.

Which leads, in short order, to a last question. Joseph Weiler, in his reflections on Europe's constitution-making, argues that the people of the cube and the people of the cathedral can coexist in a Europe that recognizes the contributions of both. Thoughtful Europeans and Americans must hope that he is right. But the question left open, a question that touches issues far beyond constitution-making, is to whom and to what each party can appeal in grounding its commitments to freedom, tolerance, and pluralism.

For their part, Europe's dwindling numbers of Christians do know (in some cases, belatedly) why they need to engage the convictions of others with respect and why they must defend the Other's freedom: because it is their Christian obligation to do so; because this is what God requires of them. But who, or what, teaches a similar sense of obligation to the people of the cube—the people for whom La Grande Arche represents a civilizational great leap forward from Notre-

Dame? Who, or what, will teach the Europeans of the future that the democratic values this cube claims to represent are worth promoting—and defending?

That is an urgent question for Europeans. It is an equally urgent question for Americans, for whom the question of the cube and the cathedral is no less central to the future of the democratic project.

Afterword to the Paperback Edition

On April 19, 2005, one of Europe's most distinguished intellectuals, Joseph Ratzinger, was elected pope, taking the name Benedict XVI. Six weeks later, in early June 2005, French and Dutch voters rejected the European constitutional treaty discussed at some length in this book. And two weeks after that, in the wake of an effective public campaign supported by the Italian Bishops Conference, Italian voters rejected new laws that would have accelerated Italy's descent into the brave new world of technologized reproduction and embryo research.

Each of these events bears on the argument of *The Cube and the Cathedral.*

There were many reasons why Cardinal Ratzinger was elected pope, but surely one of them was his brother-cardinals' concern that the collapse of Christianity in Christianity's historic heartland was having grave effects on European society and culture. Those effects are most dangerously manifest in Europe's demographic implosion, which is now undeniable. An official European Union study released in July 2005 noted that, on present trends, Europe's share of world population will drop from 12 percent to 6 percent by 2030. That same study flatly stated that "never in history has there been economic growth without population growth."

In *The Cube and the Cathedral*, I argued that Europe's willful depopulation was one expression of a crisis of civilizational morale—a crisis of many dimensions, but one that is essentially spiritual in character. In 1988, just before the Revolution of 1989 transformed European politics and created the conditions for the possibility of today's 25-member European Union, Joseph Ratzinger made a parallel point, arguing in a prescient essay that one cannot build a humane, just, prosperous, and free society on the foundations of radical skepticism about the human capacity to know the truth of anything, and radical relativism in ethics. If there are no publicly recognized moral reference points for debating the human future, then "society," as we usually understand the term, is simply impossible. However that argument played in European high culture over the ensuing seventeen years, the great majority of Ratzinger's fellow-cardinals did not seem to find his observations alarmist or excessively dour. Indeed, given the results of the conclave of 2005, it's reasonable to assume that senior churchmen from around the world think that this is precisely the message Europe—and the rest of the secularist-relativist West— needs to hear.

Then there were those French and Dutch referenda on the Euro-constitution. While it would have been satisfying to have learned that the French and Dutch electorates had rejected the constitutional treaty because the Christian sources of European culture had been obtusely omitted from the constitution's preamble, that was not the case, according to post-election exit polls and other analyses. Fears about the economic future of an enlarged E.U. operating by market principles were prominent in forging the *"Non!"* coalition in France. Continuing shock over Theo Van Gogh's murder at the hands of an Islamist extremist, and the questions that raised about E.U. multiculturalism and E.U. immigration policy, likely played a key role in the signal the Dutch voters sent to Brussels.

Thus it's not easy to conclude that the French and Dutch rejections of the Euro-constitution also marked a rejection of the distorted idea of the European project that I analyzed in *The Cube and the Cathedral*: a Europe misconceived as a thoroughly secularized public space in which transcendent moral reference points have no place in deliberations about the public good. But perhaps the French and Dutch referenda—which do seem to have thrown a large monkey wrench into the process of deepening the vertical integration of Europe, politically and legally—have created something of a pause, in which Europeans on both sides of the old iron curtain can think again about what kind of Europe they want to build. And in rethinking that question, Europeans will have a chance to revisit a related issue: Can a Europe worthy of its historic civilizational achievement be built on a foundation that excludes, from common memory and from public life, one of the moral-cultural tributaries that fed Europe's contemporary commitment to the rule of law, equality before the law, civility, tolerance, and the protection of human rights?

Pope Benedict's election, the French and Dutch referenda, and the Italian vote on reproductive technologies all intersect at this point, and on that question. Can Pope Benedict and those who share his views take

advantage of the pause that the referenda have created
to reignite the debate about the cultural foundations of
Europe and of the European Union? Benedict XVI
seems well-placed to make the effort: He is a genuinely
pan-European intellectual who speaks the continent's
principal languages and is widely respected by his
scholarly peers (as witness his membership in the
Academie Française, where he holds the chair once occupied by Andrei Sakharov). At the World Youth Day
in Cologne in August 2005, the new pope showed an
impressive capacity to fire the enthusiasm of young
adults. Might he inspire the children of the "children of
'68"—the generation responsible for turning European
secularity from a sociological datum into an ideology—
to move beyond their parents' thin concept of a democracy "neutral between worldviews"? Might Pope
Benedict's young followers demonstrate that religiously
informed moral argument can be an important component of democratic vitality?

That may seem a long shot, but one then has to take
account of the historic significance of Italy's June 2005
referendum on reproductive technology. Over the past
forty years, Italian voters have adopted laws on divorce
and abortion that were at odds with the teaching of the
Catholic Church; in both of those debates, the Church
tended to make an argument-from-religious-authority.

In 2005, the Church's leaders made a different kind of argument, a genuinely public argument, to the effect that turning human reproduction into a technological process and declaring open season on human embryos would be very bad for Italian democracy. Why? Because moves in these directions would legally reinforce two notions: that personal autonomy exhausts the meaning of human freedom, and that utility is the criterion by which the worth of human beings should be measured. The authority of the Church was not invoked; the authority of genuinely public moral argument was effectively deployed. Is there a model here for others? Can a vocabulary of the virtues—"Is it right?"—challenge, and perhaps even replace, the vocabulary of utility—"Does it work?"—in European public life? Whether Europe breaks out of its current crisis of civilizational morale has much to do with the answers to those questions.

Some will find the suggestion that the Catholic Church might be an agent of Europe's cultural renewal implausible, as some have found the argument that Christianity had a lot to do with creating the cultural conditions for the possibility of European democracy implausible. Since the publication of *The Cube and the Cathedral*, I have been regularly reminded that the European wars of religion in the sixteenth and seventeenth centuries loom as a grave warning against a European public square that is anything other than scoured of religious referents. The wars of religion surely influenced the advocates of the overthrow of the *ancien régime* on the European continent; and the various Christian communities surely have much to answer for as they remember their role in setting Europe ablaze—a role that underscores the danger to the Church of alliances with coercive state power. Yet there is a lesson here for secular democrats as well as for Christian advocates of democracy; and learning it means challenging some of the conventional wisdom about the history of modernity.

According to the conventional historiography, the Peace of Westphalia in 1648 ended the European wars of religion by endorsing the modern state system and establishing the principle of *cuius regio eius religio*—the religion of the prince would determine the religion of the people—and state power would keep religious rivalries under control. The conventional narrative (that tends to place a high value on state power) treats this as a victory for reason over passion; which, in some respects, it was. But there is another way of looking at the Peace of Westphalia. In Poland, where there were no wars of religion and where religious tolerance was generally practiced during the Reformation and Counter-Reformation, the Peace of Westphalia is typically viewed as the first moment in Europan history in which the power of the modern state was used to coerce consciences—and thus the first step along the road to the totalitarianism under which Poland suffered so grievously during the twentieth century. That analysis, I suggest, cannot be easily dismissed; at the very least, it usefully adds complexity to the conventional account. Here, once again, the "Slavic view of history" is worth reckoning with.

That having been said, however, I still doubt that the sixteenth and seventeenth century wars of religion have much to do with today's European debate, save as a form of black legend that functions as a substitute for serious historical thought. Beyond the debate over the meaning of the sixteenth and seventeenth centuries for today's Europe, however, there is the further, and more important, question of how deeply the roots of contemporary European democracy can be traced into the historical and cultural subsoil of the continent. To put it gently, it is historically unpersuasive to argue that the moral claims that gave birth to European democracy—the dignity of the human person, the superiority of the method of persuasion in politics, the limited power of the state, majority rule and the protection of minority rights—were solely the progeny of the (French) Enlightenment. So was the suggestion in the now-rejected European constitutional treaty—a suggestion informed by this implausible genealogy—that nothing of real significance for European democracy happened between Marcus Aurelius and Descartes. As for the present and future, any fair assessment of the positions will demonstrate what J. H. H. Weiler argued at the height of the Euro-constitution debate: that the Catholic Church in fact has a thicker, more compelling argument in favor of tolerance and civility than its secularist critics; so do other Christian communities who also believe it to be the will of God that (as Richard John Neuhaus once put it) they be tolerant of others who have a different view of God's will—or no view of God's will. Moreover, as the late John Paul II demonstrated with his program of "cleansing the Church's conscience" through the acknowledgment of the Church's historic sins and failures, the Catholic Church (and other Christian communities) can face, and indeed have faced, the hard truths about their pasts. But where is the "cleansing of conscience" by which European and North American "exclusive humanists" (to recall Charles Taylor's phrase) have come to grips with the slaughters unleashed when, as Aleksandr Solzehnitsyn poignantly put it, "men had forgotten God"? Where is the secularist reckoning with the "drama of atheistic humanism" described above?

On April 18, 2005, the day the conclave that would elect him pope opened, Cardinal Joseph Ratzinger, in his role as dean of the College of Cardinals, presided and preached at the Mass *Pro Eligendo Romano Pontifice* [For the Election of the Roman Pontiff]. In his homily, Ratzinger described an emerging "dictatorship of relativism that does not recognize anything as definitive and whose ultimate goal consists solely of one's ego and desires." In this new moment created by the French and Dutch rejections of the European constitutional treaty, friends of Europe can only hope that that analysis is taken seriously, and that a different kind of conversation about Europe's future follows. Can a democratic Europe coexist with a legally enforced "dictatorship of relativism" in the moral-cultural sphere? Can any democracy—European, American, or otherwise—long endure when "one's ego and desires" set the horizon of aspiration throughout society? Those are the questions the new pope is pressing; those are the questions posed by the symbols of the cube and the cathedral. On their resolution, a lot of twenty-first century history rides.

Acknowledgments

Several of the principal arguments in this book were first broached in the 2001 and 2003 William E. Simon Lectures, which I delivered at the Ethics and Public Policy Center in Washington. My best thanks to the board of the William E. Simon Foundation for their support of this lectureship. Thanks, too, to my colleagues at EPPC for their counsel and friendship.

Father Richard John Neuhaus, editor in chief of *First Things*, and Neal Kozodoy, editor of *Commentary*, opened the pages of their distinguished journals to some of the ideas developed further here. I am, as always, grateful for their friendship, encouragement, and wise editorial counsel.

While the argument of this small book is, of course, my own responsibility, I have benefited from the correspondence, conversation, and criticism of many friends and colleagues as I've developed my thinking on Europe's crisis of civilizational morale, and what it might mean for the United States, over the past several years: Frans A.M. Alting von Geusau, Stephen M. Barr, Peter L. Berger, Rémi Brague, Desmond Cardinal Connell, Midge Decter, Jean Duchesne, Hillel Fradkin, Carl Gershman, Mary Ann Glendon, Archbishop James M. Harvey, Karl Cardinal Lehmann, Daniel Johnson, Teresa Malecka, Piotr Malecki, Joachim Cardinal Meisner, Archbishop Celestino Migliore, Father Jay Scott Newman, Michael Novak, Father Edward T. Oakes, S.J., Norman Podhoretz, Christoph Cardinal Schönborn, O.P., Father Michael Sherwin, O.P., Anthony Sivers, J. H. H. Weiler, Robert Louis Wilken, Father Maciej Zięba, O.P.

Elizabeth Maguire, publisher of Basic Books, has been a constant source of encouragement and good cheer during the gestation of the three books we have now done together. My omnicompetent agent, Loretta Barrett, made it all work, as usual. Carrie Gress, Ever Johnson, Renée Gardner, and Joan Weigel were most helpful in research and in preparing the manuscript for publication.

Acknowledgments

I wrote the first draft of *The Cube and the Cathedral* in Kraków, where I have been privileged to teach every summer for the past eleven years. That experience prompted the happy thought that I might discharge part of a long-standing debt to my Cracovian friends—those in Kraków and those in Rome—by dedicating this meditation on Europe's past, present, and future, as well as its implications for America, to them. *Dziękuje bardzo.*

G.W.

9 August 2004
Memorial of St. Teresa Benedicta
of the Cross (Edith Stein),
Co-Patroness of Europe

Notes

1. Robert Kagan, *Of Paradise and Power: America and Europe in the New World Order* (New York: Alfred A. Knopf, 2003).

2. Kagan, *Of Paradise and Power*, p. 3.

3. Kagan, *Of Paradise and Power*, p. 11.

4. Cited in Kagan, *Of Paradise and Power*, p. 60.

5. Kagan, *Of Paradise and Power*, p. 61.

6. Kagan, *Of Paradise and Power*, p. 63.

7. Kagan, *Of Paradise and Power*, p. 73.

8. Kagan, *Of Paradise and Power*, pp. 73–74.

9. Josef Joffe, "The Demons of Europe," *Commentary*, January 2004, p. 31.

10. John Keegan, *The Iraq War* (New York: Alfred A. Knopf, 2004), p. 104.

11. Ian Buruma, "Mind the Gap," *Financial Times Magazine*, January 10, 2004, p. 28; Mark Steyn, "Payback Time," *Daily Telegraph*, December 14, 2003.

12. Mark Steyn, "When Irish Eyes Aren't Smiling," steynonline.com, June 15, 2004.

13. "After D-Day," *Economist*, June 12, 2004, p. 48.

14. "Europe vs. America," *Wall Street Journal*, June 18, 2004, p. A10. Economic logic is not infrequently the victim of political calculation in modern states, but certain European countries have taken the state practice of economic illogic to new extremes. Thus France spends more on "compensating" French businesses for the losses caused by the (wholly illogical) 35-hour work week than it does on its institutions of higher learning. (See Pierre Briançon, "New Bottles, Same Old Politics," *Wall Street Journal Europe*, December 16, 2004, p. A9.)

15. Pierre Manent, "Current Problems of European Democracy," *Modern Age*, Winter 2003, p. 15.

16. Rainer Zitelman, "Tabubruch Blasphemie," *Die Welt*, August 8, 1996, p. 4.

17. See Rémi Brague, *Eccentric Culture: A Theory of European Civilization* (South Bend, Ind.: St. Augustine's Press, 2002).

18. Richard John Neuhaus, "Public Square," *First Things*, March 2004, p. 66.

19. Niall Ferguson, "Eurabia?" *New York Times Magazine*, April 4, 2004.

20. Nicholas Eberstadt, "The Emptying of Russia," *Washington Post*, February 13, 2004, p. A27.

21. Fouad Ajami, "The Moor's Last Laugh," *Wall Street Journal*, March 22, 2004.

22. Phillip Longman, "The Global Baby Bust," *Foreign Affairs*, May-June 2004, p. 66.

23. Phillip Longman, *The Empty Cradle: How Falling Birthrates Threaten World Prosperity and What to do About It* (New York: Basic, 2004), p. 63.

24. Niall Ferguson, "The End of Europe?" AEI Bradley Lecture, March 1, 2004, http://www.aei.org/news20045.

25. Phillip Longman sums up the situation in these terms, with telling illustrations:

> Today, most European countries have already passed a de-mographic tipping point that virtually assures not only rapid population aging, but also absolute population de-cline. In Spain, for example, the cohort now in its infancy (ages 0–4) is more than 42 percent smaller than the cohort now in its prime reproductive years (ages 30–34). What will happen when this tiny younger generation reaches adulthood? In order to replace all members of the previous generation, each female would have to bear close to four children, as compared to the average 1.15 children pro-duced by their mothers. Since this hardly seems likely without an extraordinary transformation in both cultural values and the economic cost of children, Spain is all but fated to decline rapidly throughout at least the first half of this century. . . .
>
> According to demographer Massimo Livi-Bacci, never in the past. . . has Europe's ability to renew and sustain its population been more compromised by a dwindling supply of youth. The United Nations projects that Europe as a whole will lose 3.2 million in population between 2000 and 2005. In the following ten years, the population will de-cline by more than 11.3 million. After 2025, population loss continues compounding. Even assuming a 33 percent in-crease in fertility rates over today's levels, the U.N. proj-ects a loss of 28 million Europeans in just the 2040s.
>
> If European fertility rates remain unchanged, the only European countries that will avoid population loss by 2050, according to U.N. projections, are France, the United King-dom, Ireland, and Luxembourg, and even these countries will face rapidly aging populations. Without an increase in its fertility rate, France's working-age population (15–64) will decline by more than 9 percent by 2050, while its eld-erly population will increase by 79 percent.
>
> The financial implications are staggering. In Europe there are currently 35 people of pensionable age for every 100 people of working age. By 2050, on present demo-graphic trends, there will be 75 pensioners for every 100

workers. In Spain and Italy the ratio of pensioners to workers is projected to be one to one. Since in most major European countries pensions are financed out of current revenues, tax rates will have to soar if benefits are not cut. The Deutsche Bank calculates that average workers in Germany are already paying around 29 percent of their wages into the state pension pot, while the figure in Italy is close to 33 percent.

The social implications are also staggering. By mid-century, if current trends continue, Europe will be a society in which most adults have few biological relatives. . . .

Europe doesn't face the prospect of gradual population decline; it faces the prospect of rapid and compounding loss of population unless birthrates soon turn upward. Like population growth, population decline operates on a geometric curve that compounds with each generation. If Europe's current fertility rate of about 1.5 births per woman persists until 2020, this will result in 88 million fewer Europeans by the end of the century. To adopt a somewhat poignant metaphor: If Europe were a woman, her biological clock would be rapidly running down. It is not too late to adopt more children, but they won't look like her (*The Empty Cradle*, pp. 61–67).

26. Keegan, *Iraq War*, p. 166.

27. See Václav Havel, "The Power of the Powerless," and Václav Benda, "Catholicism and Politics," in Havel et al., *The Power of the Powerless: Citizens Against the State in Central-Eastern Europe* (Armonk, N.Y.: Sharpe, 1985).

28. Christopher Dawson, "The Outlook for Christian Culture," in *Christianity and European Culture: Selections from the Work of Christopher Dawson*, ed. Gerald Russello (Washington, D.C.: Catholic University of America Press, 1998), p. 5.

29. Aleksandr Solzhenitsyn, "Men Have Forgotten God," *National Review*, July 2, 1983, pp. 872–876.

30. Cited in Norman Davies, *Europe: A History* (New York: Oxford University Press, 1996), p. 879. Davies questions

whether Grey actually said this on the night in question, or whether he and others reconstructed the memory later. Whether Sir Edward Grey said precisely what I have just quoted on the night of August 3, 1914, as the lamplighters were turning on the lights in Whitehall, is irrelevant; the sentiment was surely Grey's, and others'.

31. Cited in David Fromkin, *Europe's Last Summer: Who Started the Great War in 1914?* (New York: Alfred A. Knopf, 2004), p. 222.

32. Fromkin, *Europe's Last Summer*, pp. 40–41.

33. Cited in Fromkin, *Europe's Last Summer*, p. 224.

34. De Lubac describes the most productive years of his varied career in a memoir, *At the Service of the Church* (San Francisco: Ignatius Press, 1993).

35. The English edition is *The Drama of Atheist Humanism* (San Francisco: Ignatius Press, 1995).

36. *Drama of Atheist Humanism*, p. 14.

37. Two theological generations after de Lubac, the Anglican Oliver O'Donovan made a similar point, if rather more densely, addressing what he termed "the nature of the impasse into which a politics constructed on an avowedly anti-sacred basis has now come. For without the act of worship political authority is unbelievable, so that binding political loyalties and obligations seem to be deprived of any point. The doctrine that *we* set up political authority, as a device to secure our own essentially private, local and unpolitical purposes, has left the Western democracies in a state of pervasive moral debilitation, which, from time to time, inevitably throws up idolatrous and authoritarian reactions." Oliver O'Donovan, *The Desire of the Nations: Rediscovering the Roots of Political Theology* (New York: Cambridge University Press, 1999), p. 49.

38. Pierre Manent, "Autumn of Nations," *Azure*, Winter 2004, p. 37.

39. Manent, "Autumn of Nations," p. 37

40. José Casanova, "Catholic Poland in Post-Christian Europe," *IWM Newsletter*, Spring 2003.

41. Christopher Dawson, "The Modern Dilemma," in *Christianity and European Culture*, p. 118.

42. At one point or another in this debate, these governments, as well as those of Austria, Germany, Greece, Hungary, Latvia, Luxembourg, and the Netherlands, indicated some degree of support for a mention in the preamble of Europe's Christian heritage. Throughout the endgame of the process, Belgium, Cyprus, Denmark, Estonia, Finland, France, Slovenia, Sweden, and the United Kingdom resisted the call to acknowledge the specifically Christian roots of European civilization. "New Row over EU Charter," *The Tablet*, May 29, 2004, p. 30.

43. Cited in *L'Osservatore Romano* (English weekly edition), July 23, 2003, p. 1.

44. Cited in "France Says No to Christianity in Constitution," euobserver.com, September 14, 2003.

45. Noted in www.religioustolerance.org/const.eu.htm.

46. www.religioustolerance.org/const.eu.htm

47. Cited in "Unholy Row on God's Place in EU Constitution," *Christian Century*, April 5, 2003.

48. "Unholy Row."

49. Cited in Gerald Owen, "Habermas + Derrida: Modernism a Beneficiary of War in Iraq," *National Post*, August 2, 2003.

50. Cited in Kamal Ahmed, "Britain to Block 'Christian Clause' in EU Constitution," *Observer*, May 9, 2004, p. 3.

51. J. H. H. Weiler, *Un' Europa cristiana: Un saggio esplorativo* (Milano: Biblioteca Universale Rizzoli, 2003). The translations below are my own, and are taken from the original Italian edition of Professor Weiler's book.

52. As did one of the greatest historians of Europe, the late Hugh Seton-Watson. In an essay published after his death in 1984, Seton-Watson offered a brisk critique of those who told the story of Europe in unilinear terms and issued a call for a more culturally textured approach to Europe: "The interweaving of the notions of Europe and of Christendom is a fact of History which even the most brilliant sophistry cannot undo. . . But it is no less true that there are strands in European culture that are not Christian: the Roman, the Hellenic, arguably the Persian, and (in modern centuries) the Jewish. Whether there is also a Muslim strand is more difficult to say." Hugh Seton-Watson, "What Is Europe, Where Is Europe? From Mystique to Politique," *Encounter*, July-August 1985, p. 16.

53. This summary is adopted from Servais Pinckaers, O.P., *Morality: The Catholic View* (South Bend, Ind.: St. Augustine's Press, 2001), p. 74.

54. Josef Pieper, *Scholasticism: Personalities and Problems in Medieval Philosophy* (South Bend, Ind.: St. Augustine's Press, 2001), p. 150.

55. Servais Pinckaers, O.P., *The Sources of Christian Ethics* (Washington: Catholic University of America Press, 1995), p. 242.

56. Pinckaers, *Sources of Christian Ethics*, p. 339. For a lengthy discussion of the freedom of indifference and its cultural consequences, see Pinckaers, *Sources of Christian Ethics*, pp. 327–353. A summary chart contrasting freedom for excellence and the freedom of indifference may be found in Pinckaers, *Morality*, p. 74.

57. On this point, see Pinckaers, *Sources of Christian Ethics*, pp. 348–349; and Pinckaers, *Morality*, p. 66. Steven Ozment discusses Kant's efforts to rescue objective morality in the context of his attempt to promote a more conservative Enlightenment in

contrast to Jacobinism, in *A Mighty Fortress: A New History of the German People* (New York: HarperCollins, 2004), pp. 180–182.

58. Peter Brown, *The Rise of Western Christendom: Triumph and Diversity,* A.D. *200–1000* (Oxford: Blackwell, 2003).

59. Brown, *Rise of Western Christendom*, p. 41.

60. Brown, *Rise of Western Christendom*, p. 6.

61. Brown, *Rise of Western Christendom*, p. 131. Brown describes the mission of "Patricius" in these ample terms: "To 'land a man on the moon'—that is, to place a Christian bishop in a totally non-Roman Ireland—showed the majestic reach of the Catholic Church, as Augustine had defined it, as a City for all nations" (*Rise of Western Christendom*, p. 130).

62. Robert Louis Wilken, "Epic of the West," *National Review*, January 26, 2004, p. 47.

63. On this point, see Peter L. Berger, "Christianity and Democracy: The Global Picture," *Journal of Democracy*, April 2004, p. 76.

64. David Warren, "Through the Eyes of Our Enemies," *Commentary*, April 2004, pp. 26–27.

65. On these and other points, see Glenn W. Olsen, *Beginning at Jerusalem: Five Reflections on the History of the Church* (San Francisco: Ignatius Press, 2004).

66. Thus Norman Davies on the pilgrimage to Compostela, one of the most popular of the Middle Ages: "At its height in the fourteenth and fifteenth centuries, the pilgrimage to Santiago was a major transcontinental business. English and Irish pilgrims often made first for Tours, or sailed to Talmont on the Gironde. The Germans and Swiss came down the Rhône to Lyons en route for Vézelay or Le Puy. Italians sailed to Marseilles or direct to Arles. Guide books were written. Abbeys and shrines on the way, such as the Abbey of Ste. Foy at Conques, grew rich from pilgrims' donations. The refuge at Roncesvalles

served 30,000 meals a year. Churchyards along the road received the remains of those who could go no further.

"Historians discuss the factors which made for the unity of Christendom. Santiago de Compostela was certainly one of them" (*Europe*, p. 278).

67. "All over Europe, tens of thousands of church parishes form a network of territorial authority, which is often much older and more continuous than that of the civil power. . . . They coincide in large measure with the village communities, where the parish priest has been a central figure of respect and influence regardless of the changes in political regime and land ownership. . . . Parish registers of births, marriages, and deaths . . . are one of the major sources of genealogical and demographic information [about Europe and its peoples]. They provide the natural gateway into local history" (Davies, *Europe*, p. 344).

68. Thus Norman Davies: "Feudalism left a profound legacy in Western culture. It molded speech and manners; it conditioned attitudes to property, to the rule of law, and to relations between the state and the individual. By its emphasis on contract, and on the balance between rights and obligations, it generated lasting concern for mutual trust and for keeping one's word. These attitudes held implications far beyond the narrow spheres of military service and land-holding" (*Europe*, pp. 315–316).

69. On this point, see the seminal essay by Richard John Neuhaus, "Can Atheists Be Good Citizens?" *First Things*, August-September 1991, pp. 17–21.

70. John Paul II, *Redemptoris Missio*, 39. Emphasis in original.

71. Congregation for the Doctrine of the Faith, *Instruction on Christian Freedom and Liberation*, p. 44.

72. On this and related acts of ecclesial repentance, as well as the theological rationale guiding them, see George Weigel,

Witness to Hope: The Biography of Pope John Paul II, rev. and exp. ed. (New York: HarperCollins, 2001), pp. 744–745, 876–877.

73. John Paul II, *Ecclesia in Europa*, 2. The text of this document may be found in *L'Osservatore Romano* (English weekly edition), July 2, 2003.

74. John Paul II, *Ecclesia in Europa*, 3.

75. John Paul II, *Ecclesia in Europa*, 4.

76. John Paul II, *Ecclesia in Europa*, 7–8.

77. John Paul II, *Ecclesia in Europa*, 9.

78. John Paul II, *Ecclesia in Europa*, 76.

79. John Paul II, *Ecclesia in Europa*, 67.

80. John Paul II, *Ecclesia in Europa*, 25.

81. John Paul II, *Ecclesia in Europa*, 25.

82. John Paul II, *Ecclesia in Europa*, 47.

83. John Paul II, *Ecclesia in Europa*, 98–99.

84. John Paul II, *Ecclesia in Europa*, 116.

85. John Paul II, *Ecclesia in Europa*, 121. John Paul II's challenge was accepted by more than a million Europeans who, by late November 2004, had signed a petition asking both the European Parliament and individual European countries to recognize Europe's Christian roots in a redrafted preamble to the European constitutional treaty. It was not clear whether the language of the preamble could be revised during the ratification process, although it was suggested that individual countries could add language to their instruments of ratification acknowledging the Christian sources of European and national culture. One evidently unhappy E.U. official remarked, of the petition campaign, "These Christians could at least have the good grace to accept that they lost the argument." (See Ambrose Evans-Pritchard, "1m Christians sign E.U. religion plea," *Daily Telegraph*, November 25, 2004.)

86. Tischner is cited in Timothy Garton Ash, *The Uses of Adversity: Essays on the Fate of Central Europe* (New York: Vintage, 1990), p. 106.

87. As observed by Mark Steyn in the *Jerusalem Post*, July 8, 2004.

88. Fouad Ajami, "The Moor's Last Laugh," *Wall Street Journal*, March 22, 2004. The brutal murder of Theo van Gogh in November 2004 graphically illustrated the emerging threat of radical Islamists within Europe—and the fragility of European civil society in the face of such threats. Van Gogh, an avant-garde Dutch filmmaker whose controversial work, *Submission*, had given great offense to Muslims, was shot down on an Amsterdam street by a twenty-six-year-old Dutch-Moroccan man, Mohammed Bouyeri, who then cut van Gogh's throat with a butcher knife before using that weapon to affix a note to the victim's chest; the note threatened further mayhem against "infidels," warned that "hair-raising screams will be squeezed from the lungs of unbelievers," and swore that Islam would "drive evil back to its dark hole using the sword." Mr. Bouyeri, who had grown up in Holland and whose Dutch was much more fluent than his Arabic, concluded his epistolary tirade in these graphic terms: "I know for sure that you, O America, are going to meet with disaster. I know for sure that you, O Europe, are going to meet with disaster. I know for sure that you, O Netherlands, are going to meet with disaster."

The van Gogh murder precipitated a series of attacks on Dutch mosques. The *Telegraaf*, a leading Dutch newspaper, editorialized that "magazines and papers which include inducements should be suppressed, unsuitable mosques should be shut down, and imams who encourage illegal acts should be thrown out of the country." Reaction was also sharp in other countries, with the German magazine *Speigel* writing that "the veil of multiculturalism has been lifted, revealing parallel societies where the law of the state does not apply."

Mohammed Bouyeri, a seemingly well-integrated member of contemporary Dutch society, had graduated from a local high school and had worked as a volunteer with young people. Thus his gruesome murder of van Gogh might well suggest a re-examination of the familiar European argument that terrorism is the product of poverty, political disenfranchisement, and similar "root causes." Like the 9/11 death pilots, Bouyeri was middle-class and reasonably well-educated—a man with prospects living in a prosperous country that prides itself on its open and tolerant society. The explanation for his behavior cannot be that Mohammed Bouyeri was one of the "wretched of the earth," protesting his disempowerment. (See Tony Blankley, "Europe to the Barricades," *Washington Times*, November 24, 2004; Glenn Frankel, "From Civic Activist to Alleged Terrorist," *Washington Post*, November 28, 2004, p. A18; Andrew Higgins, "A Brutal Killing Opens Dutch Eyes to Threat of Terror," *Wall Street Journal*, November 22, 2004, p. A1.)

89. Cited in John Allen, "The Word from Rome," e-mail news service of the *National Catholic Reporter*, June 25, 2004.

90. Ferguson, "Eurabia?"

91. Ferguson, "Eurabia?"

92. Philip Jenkins, "Godless Europe?" *Books and Culture*, May-June 2003, p. 7.

93. Opus Dei is not, technically speaking, a renewal movement but rather a "personal prelature," a kind of worldwide diocese or jurisdiction. I trust its members will permit me this functional rather than canonical description of "The Work."

94. The reconversion of Europe would also make sense of the European Union flag, those twelve gold stars on a blue field. The flag was designed by Arsene Heitz, an artist in Strasbourg, in response to a competition launched by the European Council in 1950. Heitz's design was adopted on December 8, 1955: on the Catholic liturgical calendar, the Solemnity of the Immaculate Conception of the Blessed Virgin Mary. At the time he was developing his design, Heitz, a man of deep piety, was reading a story of the apparitions of Mary at the Parisian convent of the Rue du Bac, where the "miraculous medal" devotion began.

Perhaps by coincidence, perhaps not, the traditional iconography of the Immaculate Conception (as, for example, on the miraculous medal) involves twelve stars, hearkening back to Revelation: "And a great portent appeared in heaven, a woman clothed with the sun, with the moon under her feet, and on her head a crown of twelve stars" (Revelation 12:1).

The original explanation of the design by a European Council spokesman noted that the number twelve was a "figure of plenitude," as there were not twelve members of the European Council in 1955. A current E.U. pamphlet distributed in Brussels tells a similar tale: "The European flag [is] a shared flag, blue with twelve gold stars symbolizing completeness. The number will remain twelve no matter how many counties there are in the European Union."

95. David B. Hart, "Religion in America: Ancient and Modern," *New Criterion*, March 2004, p. 6.

96. Hart, "Religion in America," p. 16.

Index

Index

Catholicism, 30, 43–48, 52, 148, 149–153. *See also* Christianity
and the French resistance to anti-Semitism, 43–48
investiture controversy in, 100–101
metaphysical boredom addressed by, 170–174
and the popularity of Pope John Paul II, 168–169
renewal among young people, 77, 151, 152–153
repentance and, 113–114
resentment against, 75–76
tolerance and, 111–112
World Youth Day of 1997, 77, 151, 152
Champs Elysées, 1
Charitable giving, 26
Charlemagne, 88, 95
Chesterton, G. K., 121
Chile, 19
Chirac, Jacques, 58–59, 140
Christianity. *See also* Catholicism; Christophobia; Judaism
atheistic humanism in rejection of, 45–48, 49–53
Byzantine, 101–102
in the Dark Ages, 94–98
in the East and the West, 94–95, 97, 101–102
Europe "made" by, 93–98, 136–137
excluded from the constitution of the European Union, 57–63, 78
future renewal in Europe, 148–153
Henri de Lubac on, 43–48
individualism in, 102–103
Joseph H. H. Weiler on European history and, 69–71
in North Africa, 155
Peter Brown on, 93–98
in Poland, 31–34, 149–150
repentance and, 113–114
replaced by paganism, 54–55
resentment against, 74–75, 76–77, 159–161
and the Revolution of 1989, 74
role in modern Europe, 122–126
as a source of European civilization, 4–5, 57–58, 99–107
tolerance and, 110–112
and the will of God, 84
Christophobia, 19–20, 27, 109. *See also* Christianity
1968 mind-set and, 73–74
as backlash to the Revolution of 1989, 74
fed by distorted teaching about European history, 76, 105–107
as reaction to the Holocaust, 73
and resentment against Christians, 74–75, 76–77
secularism and, 74–76

Churchill, Winston, 36–37, 41
City of God, The, 32
Clinton, Bill, 113
Clovis, 88
Cold War, the, 9, 24, 40, 116, 147, 158
Europe's atheistic humanism after, 50–53
Columbus, Christopher, 88
Communism, 16, 24, 49, 147
in Poland, 127–128
Comte, Auguste, 49
Constantine, 88
Cromwell, Oliver, 88
Cyprus, 56
Cyril and Methodius, 89
Czech Republic, 56, 58, 74

Dante, 89
Dark Ages, the, 95, 96
Dawson, Christopher, 32, 54–55, 94–95, 99, 106–107, 128, 137
Death in western Europe, treatment of, 20–21
Declaration of the Rights of Man and Citizen, 106
De Gasperi, Alcide, 70, 89
De Lubac, Henri, 119
on atheistic humanism, 49–53
on religion in Europe, 43–48, 55
Democracy
Christian roots of, 99–107
citizenship in, 108–109
possible future failure of European, 154–156, 175–177
Demographic suicide of western Europe, 5–6, 21–23, 132–137

Index

Index

Index

Norwid, Cyprian Kamil, 29
Notre-Dame, 2, 175–177

Odo, 90
*Of Paradise and Power:
    America and
    Europe in the New
    World Order,* 7
Ottaviani, Alfredo, 44

Paganism, 54–55
Palestinians, 16
Palestrina, Giovanni
    Pierluigi da, 90
*Pastoral Constitution on
    the Church and the
    Modern World,* 44
Patrick, apostle of
    Ireland, 90
Paul, Apostle, 90
Paul VI, 169
Péguy, Charles, 90
Peter, Apostle, 90
Pinckaers, Servais, 79,
    80, 83–84, 84
Pinochet, Augusto, 19
Pius VII, 122
Poland, 29–34, 56, 58,
    67, 74, 115–116
    Christianity in present
        day, 149–150
    Pope John Paul II's
        1979 visit to,
        129–130
    Solidarity movement
        in, 127–130
Political correctness, 26,
    113
Politics, European
    the "end of," 9–10,
        15, 19, 26–27,
        135–136, 158
    indecisiveness of, 19
    resentment against
        Christians in,
        74–75
Pornography, 25
Portugal, 56, 58
"Prester John," 90
Prodi, Romano, 9–10, 15,
    139

Promessa, 21
Prussia, 31

Qutb, Sayyid, 134

Raffaelo, 90
Ratzinger, Joseph, 113
Reagan, Ronald, 17
Redemptoris Missio, 111
Religion. *See* Christianity;
    Judaism
Repentance, 113–114
Revolution of 1989, 16,
    25, 74, 116, 128,
    173
Ricoeur, Paul, 169
*Rise of Western
    Christendom, The,*
    93–94
Roman Empire, the,
    94–96, 109
Romania, 74
Rome as the center of
    early European
    civilization, 95–96
Rouault, Georges, 90
Rublev, Andrei, 90
Russia, 31, 36, 102

Scholastica, 90
Schuman, Robert, 70, 91
Second Vatican Council,
    44, 171
Secularism, European, 27,
    49–53, 143–144,
    163–165
    Christophobia and,
        74–76
    and the constitution of
        the European
        Union, 56–68
    and the loss of hope,
        117–119
Sienkiewicz, Henryk, 29
Skepticism and relativism
    in Europe,
    110–111
Slavic view of history,
    29–34
Slovakia, 56

Slovenia, 56
Słowacki, Juliusz, 29
Social problems within
    the United States,
    25–26
Social Security, 25
Solidarity movement in
    Poland, 127–130
Soloviev, Vladimir, 29
Solzhenitsyn, Aleksandr
    on August, 1914 as the
        start of the decline
        of western Europe,
        36, 37–39, 41–42
    on forgotten God,
        33–34, 34, 36, 40,
        50
Sophia, Queen, 90
Soubirous, Bernadette, 91
Soviet Union, 16, 24–25,
    36, 116, 128
Spain, 56, 58, 147
    appeasement of
        terrorists in, 18
    birthrate in, 22
    terrorism in, 142–143
Stalin, Joseph, 74
Stanisław, 91
Stein, Edith, 147
Stephen of Hungary, 91
Stwosz, Wit, 91
Summa Contra Gentiles,
    79
Summa Theologiae, 79
Sweden, 9, 18, 21, 56
Switzerland, 116
Syria, 142

Taylor, Charles, 51
Ten Commandments, the,
    84
Teresa of Ávila, 91
Terrorism
    and the attacks of
        September 11,
        2001, 4, 6, 17,
        135, 143
    impact on the
        European Union,
        142–143
    in Spain, 18, 142–143

211

Index

Third Polish Partition, 31
Thucydides, 62
Tischner, Józef, 130
Tolerance, 110–112, 165
Turkey, 139, 141–142

Ukraine, 116
*Un'Europa cristiana: Un
  saggio esplorativo,*
  64
United Nations, the, 17,
  131, 162
United States, the
  approach to
    democracy in the
    Europe compared
    to, 3–4
  awareness of "Europe
    problem" in, 6
  confessions of faith
    among leaders of,
    165–166
  disagreements over
    Iraq between
    Europe and, 4, 5,
    140, 157–158
  and the European
    Union, 57
  freedom defined in,
    136–137
  political correctness in,
    26
  power and ideology in,
    8–9
  reasons to care about
    Europe, 131–137
  role in protecting and
    preserving Europe,
    11
  social problems within,
    25–26
  stereotypes of people
    in, 7–8

successes within the
  social framework
  of, 26
terrorist attacks of
  September 11,
  2001 on, 4, 6, 17,
  135, 143

Van Thuân, Francis
  Xavier Nguyên,
  113
Volodymyr, 91
Voltaire, 103
Von Moltke, Helmuth, 41
Von Spreckelsen, Johann
  Otto, 1

Wałęsa, Lech, 91
Warren, David, 103–104
Weiler, Joseph H. H.,
  19–20, 27, 78,
  105, 110, 176
  on the Christian
    tolerance, 111–112
  on Christophobia,
    72–77
  on the European
    Union constitution,
    64–68
  on historical memory,
    69–71, 93
Welfare reform, 26
Wesley, John, 91
Wilberforce, William, 91
Will
  and freedom, 83–86,
    136–137
  to power, 39, 49
William of Ockham,
  82–86
Włodkovic, Paweł, 91
Wojciech, Adalbert, 87

Wojtyła, Karol, 30, 44,
  117, 168, 170. *See
  also* John Paul II
Wolsey, Cardinal, 122
Woodstock, 73
World War I
  damage to European
    culture and
    civilization set in
    motion by, 41–42
  effect on the
    worldview of
    western Europe,
    9–12, 13–15
  European culture prior
    to the start of,
    37–40
  as the start of the
    decline of western
    Europe, 33–34
World War II
  effect on the
    worldview of
    western Europe,
    9–12, 13–15, 73
  French spiritual
    resistance to,
    43–48
  memorial in
    Washington, D.C.,
    35
  period after World War
    I until, 40–41, 41
  Poland during, 31
  Pope John Paul II and,
    115
Wycliffe, John, 91
Wyszyński, Stefan, 91

Youthful rebellion of
  1968, 73–74
Yugoslavia, 139

Zwingli, Huldrich, 91